SHIFT
YOUR
HABIT

SHIFT YOUR HABIT

Easy Ways to Save Money, Simplify Your Life, and Save the Planet

ELIZABETH ROGERS
with Colleen Howell, Ph.D.

THREE RIVERS PRESS
NEW YORK

Three Rivers Press and the Tugboat design are registered trademarks of
Random House, Inc.

Library of Congress Cataloging-in-Publication Data is available upon request

ISBN 978-0-307-46530-6

Printed in the United States of America

Design by Jennifer Sbranti and Lauren Dong

All photographs by Ingrid Franz Moriarty except the photograph on
page 9, by Douglas Smoot.

10 9 8 7 6 5 4 3 2 1

First Edition

For my family

CONTENTS

INTRODUCTION

The true heart and soul of living green is efficiency.

Shift Your Habit highlights the personal value that comes from living mindfully. Shifting toward a more environmentally conscious lifestyle will not only help the planet but also save you money and time, and even improve your quality of life.

Given the fiscal roller coaster we've experienced over the past few years, many of us are probably more concerned with saving money than with saving the planet. But why does it have to be either/or? Why not do both simultaneously? It turns out that the two can easily go hand in hand.

In my own experience, I've noticed that becoming greener has made my life richer and healthier and, paradoxically, less expensive. This was a revelation. Like most people, I thought going green would put a serious strain on my finances. But I found, in reality, there's no need to compromise ecological principles in order to save cash. And, perhaps surprisingly, you don't need to give up comfort, convenience, or style in order to tread more lightly on the earth.

When I wrote *The Green Book* a few years ago, I decided to focus on the scale of positive change that was possible if each person were to make a few simple lifestyle changes. Seeing how much we are capable of when we're all in it together has motivated a lot of people to think differently about their own impacts.

Now I'd like to look at these shifts from a different vantage point, and show you how they not only help the planet but also add up for you and your family as well.

Shift Your Habit is a comprehensive guide to performing everyday tasks in a smarter way. I want to spread the word that those who can benefit most from going green are people like me—people with tight budgets and busy schedules, people who want to sacrifice nothing when it comes to the health and well-being of their families. Yet despite the glut of green books and TV programs, no one seems to be speaking directly to these concerns, or in a language that resonates with mainstream America.

Shift Your Habit is for . . .

- The mom shopping at a discount store who mistakenly thinks that making environmentally responsible purchases necessarily means spending more
- The college student who, despite working two part-time jobs and belonging to his school's green coalition, thinks he can't afford to practice what he preaches
- The retired couple who live efficiently without even thinking about it—and want to continue to subsist responsibly on a fixed income
- The small-business owner who wants to cut costs and go green but doesn't know where to start
- The passionate cook who can no longer afford the ingredients he craves and wants to be able to get them locally or from his own backyard
- The single parent who is busy working and keeping the household together but still wants nothing but the best for her children

Shift Your Habit is for you.

Each entry in this book explains a seemingly small change in behavior that, over time, will make a huge difference for your family and our planet. The hundreds of simple shifts contained in this book will streamline your life and leave you with up to $50,000 or more that you thought you'd never see again. Crazy, right? I'm not preaching that you should make every shift in this book. You can pick and choose only those that fit your lifestyle, and you'll still see a huge benefit.

Regardless of your income, you probably strive to be healthy and make the most of what little time you spend not working. The lifestyle modifications in this book are virtually painless—and they will help you live better, save money, and save time. In many cases, saving the planet is an ancillary benefit—the organic, sustainable cherry on top of some sound lessons in home economics.

As a single mother living on a budget, I spend a lot of time thinking about the meaning of value. Dollars, like fossil fuels, are not a renewable resource—so I'm always looking for ways to make them go further. I also care about sustainability. I want my nine-year-old son, Emmett, to understand that even in our disposable society everything has a life cycle and that his actions have consequences. I want Emmett to have a sense of his own power—to know that his actions can help heal the planet rather than harm it.

The hundreds of shifts I propose in this book are small, but they add up. Big-time. The key to sustaining any lifestyle change is to start simple. Begin with habits that are manageable, rather than comprehensive and overwhelming. Once you achieve a consistent stream of small victories, you'll know you're moving in the right direction, and you'll be motivated to continue your progress.

Take, for example, committing to cut back on water waste. Your family is probably letting thousands of gallons of water trickle unnecessarily down the drain, but there's no need to issue an ultimatum for two-minute showers. Instead, install low-flow showerheads for just a few dollars each. They're constructed to deliver equivalent water pressure using less water, so your family won't even notice the change. You'll be saving up to $380—and 36,000 gallons of hot water—per year. And that's nothing! Wait until you hear about the shifts that could cut your food bill in half.

You can read this book cover to cover, or just flip through to the sections that you are most interested in. If you're looking for an answer to a specific question, consult the index. If you're in search of inspiration and camaraderie, check out the Swift Shifts—real-life stories from people like you who committed to implementing the shifts you'll see throughout the book and reported back about the experience.

Even if you don't think of yourself as a "green" person, you can still use this guide to streamline your life, get healthier, and save real money in the process. Before you know it, you'll be biking to work, cleaning with natural solutions, and composting from your edible garden. Don't worry—none of your friends will be able to pinpoint what's different about your life. They'll simply want to be just like you.

Moderation may not be rocket science, but it is revolutionary.

THE SHIFTERS

Once I had developed the concept behind *Shift Your Habit,* I couldn't wait to share the shifts with real people. So I set out across the country—from Huntsville to Orlando, Staten Island to Alta Dena—to find families who wanted to live thriftier, healthier, and more efficient lives. In some cases they didn't know they were looking to be greener until they met me and I charmed them into it. Okay, I'm lying. I told them I'd save them money. So how could they resist me?

I met with each family to get a sense of their needs—which elements of their lives were working well and which they felt could operate more efficiently. Then I steered them toward those shifts that seemed most pertinent given their lifestyles and let them go to town with the shifts that made most sense for them. They tell their stories and experiences with these shifts in the Swift Shifts layered throughout the book.

Each family was also challenged to make fifteen universally relevant changes that would not only provide instant environmental and economic impact but also give them the confidence to continue with this new way of living. I call these Super Shifts, because they're easy to incorporate and totally rewarding. The monetary savings listed by each Super Shift reflect actual savings realized by at least one of the Shifters.

The estimated savings quantified throughout the rest of the book are averages based on data provided by government and research institutions. For a full reference guide, visit **http://shiftyourhabit.com.**

Because your own savings may be slightly different, I encourage you to make the shifts that appeal to you—as well as a few that seem a bit more challenging—and then report your experiences at http://shiftyourhabit.com. We can calculate averages from published data until the grass-fed cows come home, but nothing beats the Shifter stories of real families like yours making real changes to benefit themselves as well as the planet.

Remember, every shift counts.

THE SUPER SHIFTS

1. Install a water filter on your kitchen faucet for easy, unlimited access to filtered water. Replace plastic bottles with reusable and refillable glass, steel, or aluminum ones.
    The Savings: $885 per year

2. Trade in paper towels for reusable cleaning cloths.
    The Savings: $130 per year

3. Trade in paper napkins for washable cloth ones.
    The Savings: $50 per year

4. Replace conventional cleaning products with natural, highly concentrated ones.
    The Savings: $85 per year

5. Pack your kids a waste-free lunch using a lunch box, thermos, and sealable containers instead of buying individually wrapped snacks, disposable lunch bags, and plastic Baggies.
    The Savings: $540 per year

6. Use a reusable canvas bag when grocery shopping.
    The Savings: 600 bags per year

7. Replace your current showerhead with a low-flow model.
    The Savings: $180 per year

8. Install faucet aerators in your bathrooms to reduce water flow and increase water pressure.
    The Savings: $30 per year

9. Put displacement bags in your toilet tanks.
The Savings: $35 per year

10. Replace your standard incandescent lightbulbs with compact fluorescent lights.
The Savings: $275 per year

11. Use rechargeable batteries instead of single-use ones.
The Savings: $60 per year

12. Shut down your computer every night.
The Savings: $55 per year

13. Instead of rinsing your dirty dishes in hot water before loading them into the dishwasher, scrape food remnants into the trash or compost bin.
The Savings: $40 per year

14. Always wash full loads of clothes and use cold water.
The Savings: $150 per year

15. Sign up for paperless billing and make online payments.
The Savings: $60 per year

In the first year, implementing these Super Shifts will require an investment of less than $200, and you'll save up to $2,575! After that, it's pure savings—and this is just the beginning!

Melissa and Michael, both of whom work full-time as health-services professionals in Huntsville, Alabama, live what many of us think of as the typical American suburban lifestyle. With three kids—Zoë, age twelve, Jackson, age five, and Cole, age four— they're on the road as much as long-haul truckers, driving to school, sports, the mall, and chain restaurants. Like many of us, they want to spend more time together doing meaningful activities and less time buying stuff and running errands.

Even though both Mike and I have always loved nature and being outside, I don't know if I ever really thought about our impact on the environment. In fact, before becoming a part of Shift Your Habit, I had never spoken to our kids about environmental issues at all. We've always been more focused on being financially responsible than ecologically responsible. I guess we had sort of taken the earth for granted.

When Elizabeth first told me about our list of shifts, I was nervous but also excited. Fortunately, most of them were easy from the beginning. We used our cloth napkins the first night we got them. I remember not wanting to get the napkins dirty. They looked so clean and pretty. When we had chicken wings for dinner, when Cole spilled his cereal on the kitchen floor—I wanted to clean up the mess with paper towels, not a pretty cloth one! Then I realized that the washing machine could make them good as new again. I don't think paper towels would fare quite as well in the washing machine.

One of the more exciting shifts we've made has involved our new backyard organic vegetable garden. The day after we planted it, I was so happy and proud of our accomplishment that I posted a blog entry titled "The Garden Is Complete." Little did I know how inaccurate this title was. Planting the seeds was just the beginning. Next came the watering and the waiting, the daily strolls through the backyard after work with Mike to look and see if anything was growing, and the excitement we both felt at the first glimpse of green pushing through the soil. Every day we have gone to check on our "baby." We have to take care of it. We replace the dirt that Max, our dog, digs up. We created a small ditch so excess water could drain away and not take our precious seeds with it.

Reflecting on the past year, I think the process of shifting has been like planting our garden. All the shifts were like seeds being planted and we're waiting and excited to see what they will grow into. Being a part of Shift Your Habit has made us so much more aware of how the choices we make impact the environment. And the fact that we're saving money is just a huge bonus! After we installed our low-flow showerhead, faucet aerators, and power strips, our electric bill last month was the lowest it has ever been.

Melissa, Huntsville, AL
Child Life Specialist
Married, Mother of Zoë, 12; Jackson, 5; and Cole, 4

HOME and GARDEN

1

It's hard to believe, but Americans stay at home an average of more than fifteen hours per weekday, and over seventeen hours per weekend day—and we surrender 35% of our incomes for the privilege. Yet somehow we've allowed ourselves to become increasingly detached from what home used to represent. We microwave processed packaged meals instead of cooking simple recipes. We dine with the television instead of with family members, and we use the dining room table to collect newspapers and junk mail. We spray bug killer on our kitchen counters instead of cleaning up the crumbs responsible for attracting the bugs in the first place. We wash our kids' clothing—and our kids!—with expensive, hard-to-pronounce potions that often leave behind more gunk than they clean off. And most of the stuff we buy is—by design—disposable.

This way of life—though it seems quintessentially "American"—is relatively new. What's funny is that the Americans who lived "greenest" had no conception of being "green" in the first place. People getting by on as little as possible—making soup out of the food scraps in their kitchens, cleaning their bathrooms with baking soda and vinegar, walking their kids to school, taking the bus to work—never dreamed of leaving the furnace or air conditioner running when they left home. I'm talking about the Greatest Generation, raised on the lessons of the Depression: our parents and grandparents. Money was tight. Resources were scarce. Virtually nothing was thrown away. I believe they're still the best source for commonsense tips on how to live healthy and save money, not to mention how to respect the world around us.

Read on for more ways to keep a green home on a budget.

INDOOR LIGHTING

Lights Out When You Are

The SHIFT: Shut off the lights when you leave a room. Seem elementary? Not for those of us who absentmindedly leave lights on in bedrooms, hallways, bathrooms, and kitchen areas, even when no one is around.

Save $$: Up to $35 per year on electricity costs, as well as the costs of bulb replacement over time.

Save the Planet: Conserve 275 kilowatt-hours of energy just by turning off a 180-watt multibulb lamp that's normally on unnecessarily for five hours per day.

Sun In

The SHIFT: If you have ample daylight coming in through the windows, open the drapes, turn off the inside lights, and let the sun illuminate your home.

Save $$: Up to $90 per year on your energy bill by turning off just five 60-watt bulbs during an eight-hour day.

Save the Planet: Save enough energy to run a flat-screen television nonstop for 24 straight weeks!

Good for You: Studies have shown that working in natural light improves comfort level and mood, making people more productive. Substantial research has also found a relation between artificial lighting—or lack of natural light—and a range of problems including depression, increased stress, headaches, afternoon tiredness, sleep disturbances, and concentration and learning difficulties.

Shift-it Tip: If you don't have access to natural lighting, consider getting a full-spectrum lamp, which mimics sunlight. It isn't quite the same as having a window, but it can be effective at reducing or eliminating some of the problems associated with artificial lighting.

A Whole New Light

The SHIFT: Replace all inefficient incandescent bulbs with an energy-efficient variety, such as compact fluorescent lights (CFLs) or light-emitting diode (LED) bulbs.

Save $$: Up to $110 per year in electricity costs.

Save the Planet: Both LEDs and CFLs are more energy efficient than incandescent bulbs, saving the average household more than 1,000 kilowatt-hours of electricity and nearly 1,600 pounds of carbon dioxide annually.

Shift-it Tip: LEDs still cost a bit more than CFLs up front, but they use less energy during operation and last three to six times longer. They also produce a more attractive and flattering light, a boon for anyone who wants to look gorgeous at home.

LIGHT BRIGHT

American households spend up to 20% of their electricity budget on lighting. If every household switched to energy-efficient bulbs, we could prevent the release of 500 million tons of carbon dioxide per year.

Unscrew Around

The SHIFT: Even though things may look a bit bare—I prefer to think of it as "minimalist"— you can cut your energy consumption significantly by disabling half of the bulbs in multibulb light fixtures.

Save $$: Up to $90 per year in electricity costs, as well as the costs of bulb replacement over time.

Save the Planet: Conserve an estimated 875 kilowatt-hours of energy by eliminating ten 60-watt bulbs that are normally on for an average of four hours per day.

Shift-it Tip: Be sure to leave enough illumination so that your eyes aren't strained.

HEATING and COOLING

Three Degrees of Separation

The SHIFT: During the winter try lowering your thermostat from 70 degrees F to 67 degrees F.

Save $$: Up to $125 on home-heating costs per year.

Save the Planet: You can reduce your heating energy consumption by up to 5% for every degree you lower your thermostat below 70 degrees F.

Shift-it Tip: If 67 degrees F feels too frigid for you, try some warmer clothing—socks and/or slippers can make a huge difference—or an extra blanket on the bed.

MAKE AN OLD-SCHOOL BED WARMER!

You'll need:

  A pair of tube socks
  About 3 pounds of flax seeds—buy them on-
    line or at your local health-food store—or
    a mixture of dry beans and rice
  Optional: a bunch of dried lavender

Fill one sock with the seeds or beans and rice (and lavender if you like), and tie in a knot. Reinforce the knot with some hand stitches. Then put the first sock, knotted side first, inside the second one, so there's little risk of spillage. You can decorate the sachet if you like (this is a fun project to do with young kids). Microwave it in one-minute increments until it's warm to the touch; then deposit it under the covers at the foot of your bed. You'll be amazed at how long it will keep your tootsies toasty—certainly long enough for you to fall into a cozy sleep. You can also drape it around your neck to relax tired muscles.

Get with the Programmable

The SHIFT: Instead of keeping the air in your home at a constant temperature no matter the time of day or night, use a programmable thermostat that automatically adjusts the temperature according to a preset timer.

Save $$: Up to $250 per year on heating and cooling costs, depending on your climate and housing characteristics.

Save the Planet: Reduce energy usage by more than 15% in the summer and by up to 25% during the winter—the same amount the average household would save by turning off the AC for four weeks during the summer *and* the heater off for a month during the winter. And incidentally—you adjust your thermostat accordingly when you go on vacation, right?

Good for You: After programming the thermostat, you won't have to worry about turning the heat down at night or turning your unit off when you leave for work. And did you know that studies show we sleep much more soundly when the air around us is cool?

Shift-it Tip: Many utility companies are now offering "smart" thermostats, which can be controlled remotely online. Check with your local energy provider about rebates and giveaways.

SWIFT SHIFT: DIAL IT DOWN

We save about $250 per year on our utility bills simply by paying attention to our thermostat. We use a programmable unit, which regulates our house's indoor temperature to get no cooler than 78 degrees F during the summer and no warmer than 68 degrees F during the winter. When we're not home, the unit is turned off completely.

Mary and Tom, Staten Island, NY
Retired Teacher and Communications Specialist

You Need Your Space (Heater)

The SHIFT: Instead of heating your entire house with a central furnace, use two or three space heaters to heat just the rooms that are occupied. After all, heating empty space is a waste of money and energy—and you'll be shocked at the heat that comes out of these little blasters.

Save $$: Up to $235 per year on home-heating costs for the average U.S. household. People with large homes in cold climates will see even bigger savings.

Save the Planet: Depending on your furnace fuel, you'll save natural gas, heating oil, or electricity, all of which are associated with greenhouse gas emissions.

Good for You: Cutting back on the time your central heater is running could extend the life of your furnace, saving you money on maintenance and eventual replacement. Just don't forget to turn the space heater off when you leave the room.

Be an Energy Star

The SHIFT: Buy an ENERGY STAR qualified air conditioner instead of a conventional unit.

Save $$: Up to $25–$150 on energy costs per year, depending on your climate and home characteristics.

Save the Planet: ENERGY STAR qualified units offer optimal energy efficiency and use about 14% less energy than standard new models.

Shift-it Tip: Air-conditioner efficiency is indicated by the seasonal energy-efficiency rating (SEER). The higher the number, the less energy a unit will use to cool your space. Look for a SEER of 14 or above. Also, be sure you buy the appropriately sized system for the space you want to cool. If you buy a unit that's too big for your room, you'll end up spending more up front, as well as more on energy to keep it running. If you buy a unit that is too small, you may save a little on the up-front purchase price, but the motor will have to work harder to maintain the desired indoor climate, increasing energy costs and possibly shortening the life of the system.

Have Your Filter

The SHIFT: Replace the air filter on your air conditioner and furnace unit every three months. Dirty air filters slow down the air intake and make the unit work harder, increasing the energy it uses.

Save $$: Up to $80 per year on heating and cooling costs.

Save the Planet: Save up to 15% of cooling energy and up to 5% of home-heating energy, for a total of up to 725 kilowatt-hours per year.

Good for You: Clean filters keep dust and grime from building up, which reduces the presence of allergy triggers as well as the need for expensive appliance repair or replacement.

Keep Your Cooler Cool

The SHIFT: Keep your air-conditioning unit out of direct sunlight to help it work more efficiently and save energy.

Save $$: Up to $40 on home-cooling costs per summer.

Save the Planet: A shaded air conditioner can use 10% less energy than one operating in the sun.

Shift-it Tip: You can plant trees or shrubs to shade your AC unit. Just make sure to leave enough clearance and remove any brush so as not to block the flow of air.

Number-One Fan

The SHIFT: In warm climates, fans may not be a viable substitute for AC, but they can allow you to set your thermostat a couple of degrees higher without losing comfort. Using fans in conjunction with your air conditioner is a great way to cut down on energy costs.

Save $$: Up to $30 per summer on home-cooling costs by using a fan and raising your thermostat by 4 degrees F.

Save the Planet: Save 1% to 3% of your AC energy usage for every degree the thermostat is raised above 72 degrees F.

Good for You: Reducing air-conditioner usage can help extend the life of the unit, delaying the need to eventually replace it.

Be Shady

The SHIFT: Shade your windows to keep the heat out during the summer and in during the winter.

Save $$: Up to $210 per year on heating and cooling costs.

Save the Planet: Reduce energy usage by up to 33% for air-conditioning and 10% for heating. Combined, your electricity and natural gas savings could reduce carbon dioxide emissions by more than 2,500 pounds per year.

Shift-it Tip: If you're in the market for new drapes or blinds, choose a light color—which reflects light instead of absorbing it—and a closed-weave fabric. Hang window coverings as close to windows as possible, and allow them to touch the windowsill or floor.

Weather or Not

The SHIFT: Use caulking and weather stripping to seal tiny gaps and cracks around your doors and windows that allow outside air to come inside.

Save $$: Up to $120 per year on heating and cooling costs.

Save the Planet: Conserve at least 10% of home energy used for heating and cooling—equivalent to going three weeks without AC during the summer and two weeks without heat in the winter.

Stellar Savings

Here's what you'll save annually by choosing ENERGY STAR qualified appliances in lieu of conventional ones. You could also receive a tax credit of up to $1,500 for purchasing certain energy-efficient products.

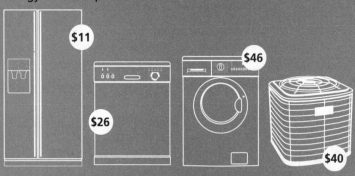

CONVENTIONAL APPLIANCE				
APPLIANCE	INITIAL COST	ANNUAL ENERGY USE	ANNUAL WATER USE	ANNUAL OPERATING COSTS
Refrigerator	$1,070	670 kWh	—	$71
Dishwasher	$545	264 kWh 19 therms	1,290 gals.	$58
Clothes washer	$300	82 kWh 30 therms	12,800 gals.	$104
Central air conditioner	$1,126	3,517 kWh	—	$387
Central furnace	$780	667 therms	—	$847
Room air conditioner	$270	1,561 kWh	—	$165
Air purifier	$143	596 kWh	—	$63
Ceiling fan	$190	269 kWh	—	$28
Gas water heater	$518	283 therms	—	$380

Check out www.energy.gov/taxbreaks.htm for more information on federal tax incentives for energy-efficiency projects.

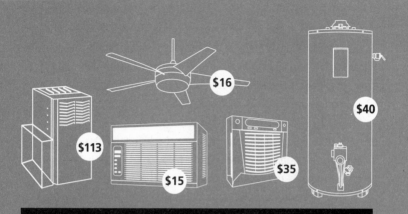

ENERGY STAR QUALIFIED APPLIANCE

INITIAL COST	ANNUAL ENERGY USE	ANNUAL WATER USE	ANNUAL OPERATING COSTS	NET ANNUAL SAVINGS
$1,100	570 kWh	—	$60	$11
$545	187 kWh 6 therms	860 gals.	$31	$26
$500	20 kWh 30 therms	5,800 gals.	$58	$46
$1,219	3,153 kWh	—	$347	$40
$1,100	578 therms	—	$744	$113
$300	1,417 kWh	—	$150	$15
$200	329 kWh	—	$35	$28
$276	117 kWh	—	$12	$16
$589	217 therms	—	$340	$40

Open Up

The SHIFT: Take advantage of cool air during summer nights by turning off the AC and opening your windows when the sun sets. Just close them in the morning when it starts to heat up.

Save $$: Up to $130 on home-cooling costs per summer.

Save the Planet: Depending on how much you typically run your air conditioner at night during warm months, you could save 1,230 kilowatt-hours or more per summer.

Good for You: Opening your windows occasionally can improve indoor air quality by clearing out toxins that linger in the air from personal care products; cleaners; and any glues, paints, or finishes on products in your home that off-gas volatile organic compounds.

Shift-it Tip: Install a window fan to offset the humidity—you'll be amazed at what a difference it makes.

Put a Damper on It

The SHIFT: Close the fireplace damper when there's no fire burning. Doing so will prevent your home's heated or conditioned air—not to mention your energy dollars—from escaping up the chimney.

Save $$: Up to $70 per year on heating and cooling costs.

Save the Planet: Closing an open damper could save about 8% of the energy used to heat your home during the winter.

Shift-it Tip: Make sure no smoldering embers are lingering in the fireplace before you close the damper, or your entire evening could go up in smoke. If you don't have a damper or choose not to use the fireplace at all, consider using a piece of rigid insulation (purchased inexpensively from the hardware store) or an inflatable stopper to block off the chimney.

Log Story

The SHIFT: Burn fire logs (preferably ones made from bio-wax, saw-dust, or other plant matter) in your fireplace instead of wood.

Even $$: Prices can be comparable.

Save the Planet: Fire logs contain more energy per pound and emit 70% to 90% less toxic pollution than wood. Plus, for the amount of heat given off, fire logs emit one-third the carbon dioxide emissions of wood.

Good for You: Fire logs are better for your health because they produce less air pollution. They're almost ash-free, so there's no messy cleanup job to tackle the next day.

WATER HEATER

Water Down

The SHIFT: Lower the thermostat setting on your water heater from 140 degrees F to 120 degrees F.

Save $$: Up to $70 per year for an electric water heater, and up to $40 or more per year for a gas water heater.

Save the Planet: For every 10 degree F reduction, you can conserve 3% to 5% of the energy used by your water heater.

Good for You: Lower temperatures reduce not only the risk of scalding but also reduce corrosion and mineral buildup in your tank and pipes, which could extend the life of your water heater.

Warm Your Heater

The SHIFT: If your water heater tank is warm to the touch, you can reduce heat losses by insulating it with a water heater blanket. Just don't put the blanket anywhere near the pilot light!

Save $$: Up to $55 per year for electric water heaters and up to $35 per year for gas water heaters.

Save the Planet: Insulating a warm tank can reduce energy usage by 4% to 9%.

Shift-it Tip: Follow the instructions on your water heater or visit the U.S. Department of Energy website for information on how to safely and effectively insulate your water heater (www.energysavers .gov/your_home/water_heating/index.cfm/mytopic=13080).

Dial It Down When Out of Town

The SHIFT: Set your water heater to the lowest temperature—or to the "vacation" setting—when leaving town for more than three days.

Save $$: Up to $10 for a gas water heater and up to $15 for an electric water heater for every month you're away.

Save the Planet: Conserve the natural gas or electricity that would otherwise have been consumed to keep water in the tank warm even when no one is home to use it.

Good for You: Discourage squatters from seeking hot showers while you're gone.

CLEANING

Play Kitchen Chemist

The SHIFT: Replace your standard household cleaning products with home remedies—just like the ones your grandma used.

Save $$: Up to $200 per year.

Save the Planet: Avoid exposing your family—and our groundwater—to tons of toxic substances.

A CLEANER CLEANER

Here's a recipe for a 100% natural window cleaner. Mix the following ingredients in a spray bottle:

1½–2 cups water
½ cup white or apple cider vinegar
¼ cup rubbing alcohol (70%)
1–2 drops lavender, cinnamon, clove, or orange essential oil

Use this mixture—which costs about 25 cents to make—to clean all your glass surfaces. Extra credit for using newspaper, which won't leave lint or consume trees, instead of paper towels.

Au Naturel

The SHIFT: If you can't be bothered to make your own potions, opt for natural cleaners instead of traditional ones containing chlorine, ammonia, or other caustic chemicals.

Save $$: Natural cleaners may appear to cost a bit more than conventional ones, but they're usually more concentrated. So if you dilute them according to the directions, you could save money in the long run—up to $100 per year.

Save the Planet: Natural cleaners use plant-based surfactants instead of petroleum or petrochemical ones. They're chlorine-, phosphate-, and fragrance-free and often are labeled "non-toxic." Fewer chemicals in the environment means less environmental pollution from their manufacture, use, and disposal.

Good for You: These products are just as effective at cleaning as standard household products, but they don't pollute your home in the process.

These Oils Are Essential

The SHIFT: Use essential oils like thyme, eucalyptus, and lavender as effective nontoxic alternatives to the petroleum-based disinfectants used in commercial cleaners.

Even $$: Prices can be comparable.

Save the Planet: Keeping toxic cleaners out of your home reduces the production of the chemicals used to manufacture those cleaners, as well as their eventual disposal in the environment.

Shift-it Tip: Mix 20 drops of essential oil (thyme, eucalyptus, or lavender work best) with 1 cup of water in a spray bottle. Shake solution and spray infected area. Let sit for at least fifteen minutes before rinsing, or don't rinse at all to let the scent linger.

TOO MUCH CLEANING CAN BE DIRTY

A study conducted by the U.S. Environmental Protection Agency found that air quality in U.S. homes is five to ten times more toxic than the air outside. Indoor air is typically contaminated by anywhere between 20 and 150 different pollutants, most of which come from petroleum-based cleaners. The bottom line is, you spend a lot of time cleaning—about 350 hours per year, using about 25 gallons of household cleaning products. Now this isn't to say that you should necessarily clean less often. But it's important that whatever you're up to your elbows in is safe to touch and breathe. Would you take a shower in glass cleaner?

Homemade Cleaners

More recipes for healthy homemade cleaners:

	All-Purpose Cleaner	Disinfectant All-Purpose Cleaner	Glass Cleaner	Oven/Stove Cleaner	Toilet Cleaner	Bathroom Tile Cleaner
Water	8 cups	2 cups	1½ –2 cups	1 tbsp.		½ cup
White vinegar	½ cup		½ cup		1 cup	
Baking soda	¼ cup			2 tbsp.	¼ cup	
Borax						
Lemon juice						
Olive oil						
Salt						
Hydrogen peroxide						¼ cup
Castile soap		3 drops				
Rubbing alcohol (70%)			¼ cup			
Dried herbs (lavender, basil, rosemary)						
Essential oil (lavender, cinnamon, clove, orange, eucalyptus)		30 drops lavender essential oil	1–2 drops			
Directions Key # (page 30)	1	2	3	4	5	6

Soap Scum Remover	Drain Cleaner	Carpet Stain Remover	Carpet Deodorizer	Wood Furniture Polish	Fabric Softener
¼ cup	8 cups				
	1 cup	¼ cup	1 cup		½ cup
½ cup	1 cup				
		¼ cup		2 tbsp.	
				¼ cup	
		¼ cup			
			¼ cup		
7	8	9	10	11	12

continues

Homemade Cleaners

Directions Key (see pages 28–29)

Recipe #	Directions
1	Mix in spray bottle. Good for hard-water stains. Can be stored for later use.
2	Mix in spray bottle. Use on any surface (countertop, toilet, tile, even in kids' rooms).
3	Mix in spray bottle. Use to clean all glass surfaces or mirrors. Use newspaper instead of paper towels if possible.
4	Mix ingredients in bowl or jar. Apply paste to spill spots. Let sit for 2 hours. Wipe up with sponge or scrub with old toothbrush.
5	Mix ingredients in bowl or jar. Pour into toilet. After 3 minutes, scrub with brush and flush.
6	Mix in spray bottle. Spray on areas with mold and leave on for at least 1 hour before rinsing.
7	Mix ingredients to make paste. Use to scour away soap scum with clean sponge, cloth, or bristle brush.
8	Pour baking soda down the drain followed by the vinegar. Let sit for 5 minutes. Flush down with near-boiling water.
9	Mix in bowl or jar. Rub paste into carpet and let dry. Then vacuum.
10	Mix ingredients in flour sifter and sprinkle around room. Vacuum after 30 minutes.
11	Mix and apply to clean cotton cloth. Use wide strokes to polish wood surface.
12	Add to rinse cycle in place of liquid fabric softener.

Throw in the Towels

The SHIFT: Buy a reusable cleaning cloth instead of using rolls (and rolls) of paper towels.

Save $$: Up to $150 per year for a household that uses two rolls per week.

Save the Planet: Conserve up to 30 pounds or more of tissue-grade paper, which is made from trees, manufactured using hundreds of gallons of water, and treated with harsh chemicals and bleach. You'll also keep this paper waste from entering the landfill.

SWIFT SHIFT: REALLY CLEAN

Because I was concerned about the chemicals I was exposing my kids to by using conventional cleaners, I was eager to try making some household cleaning recipes myself. I couldn't believe how well these mixtures actually work! Even though there was a small explosion involving some baking soda and vinegar, I got everything under control pretty quickly. Considering the health factor, and the fact that we're saving about $200 per year, I don't see us buying commercial cleaning products ever again.

Melissa, Huntsville, AL
Child Life Specialist
Married, Mother of Zoë, 12; Jackson, 5; and Cole, 4

Trickle-Down Cleaning

The SHIFT: When you're doing a thorough cleaning, start at the top of a room and work your way down.

Even $$: Prices can be comparable.

Good for You: Cleaning from the top down will give your house a more thorough cleaning—especially with respect to dust—

which can significantly improve allergy symptoms and decrease how frequently you need to clean. Plus, it's much less frustrating to clean this way.

BUYER BEWARE

If your favorite household cleaner contains any of the following ingredients, put it back on the shelf. In addition to being highly toxic if inhaled or swallowed, these chemicals can cause serious damage in other ways:

Ammonia—Skin contact may cause burns. Repeated exposure may harm the liver, kidneys, and respiratory system.

Chlorine bleach (sodium hypochlorite)—A skin, eye, and respiratory irritant. Repeated exposure may impact the immune, blood, heart, or respiratory systems.

Formaldehyde (formalin, urea formaldehyde, phenol formaldehyde)—Toxic if absorbed through the skin or inhaled. Is linked to cancer of the nose and throat in humans.

Lye (sodium hydroxide, caustic soda)—Skin contact may cause burns. Exposure to certain metals can produce hydrogen gas, which is a fire hazard.

Hydrochloric acid (hydrogen chloride)—Exposure can burn or irritate eyes, skin, nose, and respiratory tract.

Nonylphenol ethoxylates—Breaks down in the environment into a highly toxic by-product, which severely impacts wildlife.

Eschew Shoes

The SHIFT: Keep outside dirt, grime, and toxins away from your living space by adopting a no-shoes-indoors policy.

Save $$: Up to $10 per year on cleaning products.

Save the Planet: By reducing the frequency with which you have to dust, sweep, vacuum, and mop, you'll be saving both resources and energy.

Good for You: Save 25 hours per year or more by cutting your cleaning routine by a half hour per week. Floors and carpets will look newer longer, postponing the need for deep-cleaning and/or eventual replacement. You may find your health improves as well, especially if you live in an area with high levels of dust, pollen, or other allergy triggers.

Shift-it Tip: Wear lightweight slippers or socks as opposed to walking barefoot indoors. Walking barefoot can lead to carpet stains and premature wear as dust and dirt mix with oils on the soles of the feet.

SWIFT SHIFT: LETTING IT ALL SINK IN

It was a small moment of triumph when I washed my hands in the kitchen sink and used the cloth towel Jill had strategically placed, instead of a wad of paper towels. Talk about teamwork!

And Jeremy was so intrigued by the natural cleaning products that he even offered to help me clean the house. We don't even mind turning our plastic zipper-top bags inside out and reusing them, or washing our tinfoil. Since we were supposed to get rid of them altogether, using them at all feels like a luxury.

We can't believe how much money we're saving! Just by switching our cleaning routine and giving up paper towels for cloth ones we're all set to save more than $400 this year!

Jill and Jeremy, Orlando, FL
Medical Administrator and Realtor
Pet Lovers and Parents-to-Be

No-Pet Zone

The SHIFT: Keep doors closed to areas of the house your pets shouldn't frequent—especially if they are indoor–outdoor animals.

Save $$: Up to $10 per year on cleaning products.

Save the Planet: Reducing the total area in which you have to dust, sweep, and vacuum pet hair and dander results in both resource and energy savings.

Good for You: Save 25 hours per year or more by cutting your cleaning time by one-half hour per week.

POWER PLANTS

Get live plants for your house instead of artificial plants made from silk or plastic. Live plants improve indoor air quality by filtering out airborne toxins and hazardous gases. Unlike fake plants, live plants rarely require dusting, saving you (or your housekeeper) a few hours of tedious cleaning per year.

NASA has suggested that the following eleven plants are most effective at removing indoor air pollution:

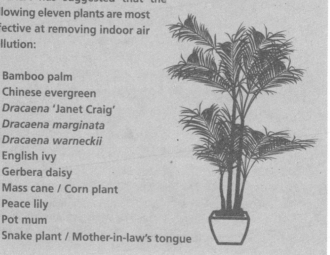

Bamboo palm
Chinese evergreen
Dracaena 'Janet Craig'
Dracaena marginata
Dracaena warneckii
English ivy
Gerbera daisy
Mass cane / Corn plant
Peace lily
Pot mum
Snake plant / Mother-in-law's tongue

KITCHEN

Remodel

The SHIFT: If your kitchen is sporting a refrigerator model from the 1970s or '80s, consider retiring it and buying a new one.

Save $$: Up to $185 per year in energy costs.

Save the Planet: New refrigerators can use less than one-fifth the energy used by old ones, so replacing an outdated fridge could save enough energy to run your new refrigerator for more than four years. Further, new refrigerators use coolants that are safer for the environment than the ozone-destroying chlorofluorocarbons used in old models.

Shift-it Tip: Many utility companies offer monetary incentives of up to $50 or more if you retire an old refrigerator. They'll even come pick it up for free.

Spare the Spare

The SHIFT: If you're using a spare fridge just to hold sodas, beer, or other essentials that could as easily be stored in a cupboard or on a shelf, consider retiring it.

Save $$: Up to $250 per year on energy costs if your fridge was made prior to 1980.

Save the Planet: Refrigerators are among the most energy-intensive appliances in the home, and older ones are less efficient than newer ones. Getting rid of your old extra fridge could save up to 2,500 kilowatt-hours of energy per year.

Suck It Up

The SHIFT: Keep your refrigerator coils from getting caked with dust and grime by brushing or vacuuming them every six months.

Save $$: Up to $35 per year.

Save the Planet: Cleaning your refrigerator coils—which dissipate heat generated by the motor—will help your refrigerator run more efficiently, saving energy over time.

Shift-it Tip: For those of you who don't know what refrigerator coils are, much less how to clean them, here's a primer. These coils cool the air in the fridge, and they are located at the bottom of the front of the fridge, under a panel (or "kick plate") that covers them. To clean them, unplug the fridge, remove the panel, and use the hose attachment on your vacuum to suck out all the caked-on dust and grime. Prepare to be horrified.

Not-So-Deep Freeze

The SHIFT: Raise your refrigerator temperature from 34 degrees F to 37 degrees F and your freezer temperature from -3 degrees F to 0 degrees F.

Save $$: Up to $10 per year on energy costs.

Save the Planet: Save up to 90 kilowatt-hours of electricity annually.

Good for You: Avoid inadvertently freezing items stored near the back of the fridge.

Closed-Door Policy

The SHIFT: Don't linger with indecision in front of an open fridge.

Save $$: Up to $10 in electricity costs per year.

Save the Planet: Conserve up to 85 kilowatt-hours of electricity per year—as much energy as the average fridge draws over the course of nearly two weeks.

Don't Blow Your Gasket

The SHIFT: Make sure your refrigerator and freezer door gaskets are tightly sealed. Otherwise, your refrigerator is working to cool the air in the kitchen in addition to cooling the contents of the fridge.

Save $$: Up to $10 per year.

Save the Planet: Replacing leaky gaskets keeps the cold air in and the warm air out, reducing the amount of energy consumed by your appliance.

Shift-it Tip: What's a gasket? you ask. It's the rubber lining that creates a seal between the refrigerator and its doors, so cold air can't escape. A good way to test the tightness of your gaskets is to see whether you can slide a slip of paper past them when the fridge door is shut. If you can, you've got loose gaskets and should look into replacing them.

Water Down

The SHIFT: If you wash dishes by hand, don't let the water run continuously. Instead, use one side of your sink for washing and fill up the other side for rinsing. If you don't have a two-sided sink, buy a plastic tub for washing.

Save $$: Up to $85 per year on water and energy costs if you have a gas water heater and up to $115 if you have an electric one.

Save the Planet: If you wash dishes by hand for 20 minutes four times per week, you could save up to 8,300 gallons of water or more per year by keeping your faucet turned off while you wash. Assuming you're washing and rinsing in hot water, you'll also save over 40 therms of natural gas or 775 kilowatt-hours of electricity—as much energy as the average household's water heater consumes over seven months.

Hire a Dishwasher

The SHIFT: Don't waste your time and money washing dishes by hand if you have a working automatic dishwasher.

Save $$: Up to $55 on water and energy bills per year (even after accounting for the electricity used by the dishwasher).

Save the Planet: Save roughly 5,000 gallons of water, as well as the gas or electric energy used to heat it.

Good for You: Save up to 230 hours per year—nearly ten days—of dishwashing time.

Throw the Rinse down the Drain

The SHIFT: Don't prerinse dishes before loading them into the dishwasher. Just scrape excess food remnants into the trash—or, even better, your compost bin. (Note: Meats, oils, and animal fats should not be composted.)

Save $$: Up to $35–$45 per year on water and water-heating energy costs.

Save the Planet: Save an average of 4,300 gallons of water per year. If warm or hot water is used, save up to 20 therms of natural gas or 400 kilowatt-hours per year.

Shift-it Tip: If you want to avoid dried-on food or have fear that rotting food will smell up your dishwasher, just run the "rinse only" cycle. It uses a tiny fraction of the water you'd use rinsing your dishes by hand under the faucet and still saves the time you'd spend standing over the sink.

Load It Up

The SHIFT: Instead of running your dishwasher every day when it's only half filled, run it every other day when the racks are full.

Save $$: Up to $25–$30 per year on water, energy, and dishwasher detergent costs by cutting dishwasher use in half.

Save the Planet: Save more than 1,100 gallons of water as well as enough electricity and hot-water energy to run your dishwasher for an entire year.

Good for You: Spend less time unloading.

Air Is Free

The SHIFT: Instead of using the heat-dry setting on your dishwasher, let your dishes air-dry.

Save $$: Up to $10 per year on electricity costs.

Save the Planet: Deactivating the heat-dry setting can save 15% to 50% of the dishwasher's electricity use—or roughly 90 kilowatt-hours per year.

Shift-it Tip: If you don't have a way of turning off the heat-dry feature, just turn off the dishwasher after its final rinse and open the door. Put your face up to it for a steamy impromptu facial.

Trash the Bags

The SHIFT: Instead of buying trash can liners, use old grocery bags for your garbage. Use trash liner bags only for waste containers that cannot be cleanly emptied directly into the garbage bin.

Save $$: Up to $35 per year if you eliminate plastic trash bags altogether.

Save the Planet: Save up to 3 pounds of plastic waste, as well as the petroleum and chemicals used to make the plastic.

Shift-it Tip: Save time shopping for trash can liners—and stop feeling guilty when you come home with a car full of grocery bags. Make use of them! If you're eliminating liners from wastebaskets, don't forget to wipe their insides down once a week, and spray with the essential-oil-and-water mixture mentioned earlier to control any undesirable smells.

BATHROOM

Shower Power

The SHIFT: Use an ultra-low-flow showerhead, which uses 1.5 gallons per minute, instead of a standard showerhead, which uses 2.5 gallons per minute.

Save $$: Up to $135 per year in water and water heating costs for a family of four with an electric water heater. You could save more than $100 if you have a gas water heater.

Save the Planet: Save 12,000 gallons of water and up to 1,250 pounds of carbon dioxide from water heating energy saved per year.

Don't Throw In the Towel

The SHIFT: If you and your family are in the habit of using a fresh towel after every shower, consider whether this is necessary. You are clean when you emerge from the shower, right? So why not hang the towel to dry and use it a few more times before washing it?

Save $$: For a family of four, save up to $105 per year on water, energy, and laundry detergent costs if laundry is reduced by just two loads per week.

Save the Planet: Conserve 3,400 gallons of water, 50 therms of natural gas, and 410 kilowatt-hours of energy.

Good for You: Eliminate the time it takes to wash, dry, and fold an additional 105 loads of laundry per year, assuming each load holds 12 bath towels.

Shorter Shower

The SHIFT: Shorten your shower by two minutes per day.

Save $$: Up to $80 per year in water heating and water costs for a family of four.

Save the Planet: Save 7,300 gallons of water and about 25 therms of natural gas—equivalent to the amount of total energy your water heater uses over nearly two months.

Good for You: You'll also save a couple of minutes per day—a total of 12 more hours per year.

Plug Plug

The SHIFT: If you're a bath taker, plug the drain before turning on the water.

Save $$: Up to $15 per year if water from the tub faucet runs down the drain for two minutes less per day.

Save the Planet: Save 3,650 gallons of water per year or more.

VS.

Which is greener? A SHOWER or a BATH?

The average tub holds 42 gallons of water but fancy models can be twice as big. Here's how the amount of water you use in the shower compares with filling up the bathtub.

Shower time (minutes)	2	4	6	8	10	12	14	16
Water use (gallons)	5	10	15	20	25	30	35	40

Shower time (minutes)	18	20	22	24	26	28	30	35
Water use (gallons)	45	50	55	60	65	70	75	80

Collect Shower Drops

The SHIFT: Use a bucket to catch water in the shower while you're waiting for it to heat up. Then use it to water your plants.

Save $$: Up to $3 per year if you save 2 gallons per day.

Save the Planet: Conserve about 730 gallons of water per year.

Good for You: You'll get some serious exercise lugging all that water around. Just be sure not to strain your back.

Leak Show

The SHIFT: Fix your constantly running or leaky toilet.

Save $$: If you have a serious leak, fixing it with a new flapper valve can save you up to $60 per month.

Save the Planet: Save up to 500 gallons of water per day.

Shift-it Tip: To check for a leaky toilet, add a few drops of food coloring to the tank. Don't flush the toilet for at least 30 minutes. If the color in the tank shows up in the bowl, you've got a leak.

Royal Flush

The SHIFT: The next time you replace your toilet, buy a high-efficiency-toilet (HET) model, which uses 1.28 gallons of water per flush or less, instead of a standard toilet, which uses 3.5 gallons per flush.

Save $$: Up to $70 per year in water costs for a family of four. Plus, many HETs qualify for cash rebates. Usually provided by water utilities, these can be as much as $150 per unit.

Save the Planet: Conserve nearly 18,000 gallons of water per year.

Shift-it Tip: Some communities offer recycling programs for old sinks and toilets. The porcelain is crushed and used in a road base for street and highway paving.

SWIFT SHIFT: LEAK HOUSE

The first day of shifting was kind of discouraging. My apartment was old and drafty and everything leaked, but my roommates were too busy to even listen to what I wanted to change. Some agreed to help, but they didn't have time to do anything more than sort the recycling. So I took matters into my own hands. I tightened the fittings on the showerheads with a wrench so they no longer leaked. I also fixed the toilet that was running constantly. I thought the dripping sink faucet was unfixable until I discovered the two knobs under the sinks that allowed me to shut the water off. No more drips. I was so empowered by this experience. I was no longer a victim to bad plumbing, and it didn't matter that my roommates weren't on board. I took care of it myself and, according to Elizabeth's calculations, am keeping about 13,000 gallons of water from being wasted per year!

Christin, Glendale, CA
Television Producer and Vintage Clothing Entrepreneur, Single, 28

Get Tanked

The SHIFT: If you have an older toilet that uses more than 1.6 gallons per flush, try using this MacGyver method to minimize water use: Buy a tank displacement bag or fill a half-gallon glass or plastic bottle with water (don't use a brick) and then place it in the toilet tank away from the moving parts. The half gallon of water you displace in the tank will be saved every time you flush.

Save $$: Up to $35 on water and sewage costs per year for a family of four—even if no one flushes less than normal.

Save the Planet: Conserve nearly 8,700 gallons of water per year.

Mellow Yellow

The SHIFT: "If it's yellow, let it mellow. Flush it down if it's . . ." You get the picture.

Save $$: Up to $40 per year on water and sewage costs if everyone in a family of four flushed twice less per day with a 3.5-gallon-per-flush toilet.

Save the Planet: Save more than 10,000 gallons of water per year.

Shift-it Tip: If you teach your kids to let it mellow at home, it's important to explain that it's not appropriate to do so in public restrooms or when visiting other people's homes.

SWIFT SHIFT: FEELING FLUSH

Seeing the kids adjust to these changes has been so funny. Mike spoke with the boys about not flushing the toilet every time they pee, explaining that every flush costs money. He also explained, in a way a three- and five-year-old would understand, how important it is to turn the lights off. "The more money we spend on water and electricity, the less we'll have to spend on candy." A couple of days later, Cole, the four-year-old, went to the bathroom and flushed. I could hear Jackson yelling "Cole! Don't flush it, that's our candy money!"

Melissa, Huntsville, AL
Child Life Specialist
Married, Mother of Zoë, 12; Jackson, 5; and Cole, 4

Don't Give Your Brushes the Brush-off

The SHIFT: Avoid buying those disposable toilet brushes with which you reuse the plastic handle and use a new disposable brush each time you clean. The traditional reusable plastic brush works fine. Just rinse it in the clean toilet water when you're finished scrubbing and store it behind the toilet in a designated container.

Save $$: Up to $50 per year if the toilet is cleaned once a week.

Save the Planet: Avoiding disposable toilet brushes, whether they're the flushable or throw-away variety, keeps unnecessary waste from piling up in landfills across the country.

Don't Flush Your Trash

The SHIFT: Dispose of trash in a wastebasket, not in the toilet.

Save $$: Up to $20 per year if the toilets in your home are flushed four times less per day.

Save the Planet: Conserve 5,100 gallons of water or more per year. If you're concerned about this tip generating additional landfill waste, there's no need to worry. Any solid waste that ends up at the sewage treatment plant is ultimately shipped to a landfill anyway. So by throwing bathroom refuse in the trash instead of into the toilet, you're bypassing the wastewater treatment step of the waste disposal process.

On a Roll

The SHIFT: Buy six 4-in-1 giant rolls of toilet paper instead of 24 single rolls (six 4-packs).

Save $$: Up to $55 per year for a family of four.

Save the Planet: Save a half pound of landfill waste (from having fewer cardboard rolls to throw away) and 1.5 cups of diesel fuel from less packaging and transport costs.

Good for You (and lazy family members): Save time! Change your roll less often.

Not So Hot

The SHIFT: Make it a habit to use only the cold-water faucet unless you specifically want hot water. If you turn on the hot water when you wash your hands or brush your teeth, for example, chances are that the water won't even be hot by the time you're finished, but you've still paid to heat it.

Save $$: Up to $70 per year in energy savings for a family of four that routinely uses the cold-water faucet in the bathroom instead of the hot-water faucet.

Save the Planet: Conserve 675 kilowatt-hours of water heating energy, and reduce carbon dioxide emissions by 1,045 pounds per year.

Shave Off a Few Gallons

The SHIFT: Turn the water off while you're shaving.

Save $$: Up to $25 in water and energy costs per year for each daily shaver in the household.

Save the Planet: Save 1,825 gallons of water as well as water heating energy.

Turn It Off

The SHIFT: Turn the water off while you brush your teeth.

Save $$: Up to $20 per year on water costs for a family of four brushing twice a day.

Save the Planet: Save 1,400 gallons of water per year per person who turns off the water instead of leaving the faucet running through the entire brushing routine.

Air to Spare

The SHIFT: Replace your current faucet aerator—the cylindrical metal tube that threads onto the end of the faucet—with a low-flow aerator rated at 0.5 gallons per minute (gpm).

Save $$: Up to $15 per year on water costs for a family of four. If hot water is being used, save an additional $35 per year on energy expenditures.

Save the Planet: Conserve up to 3,650 gallons of water per year.

Good for You: Lower water pressure means water is less likely to spray all over the bathroom.

BEDROOM

Don't Count Sheets

The SHIFT: Choose 300-count sheets instead of 600-count sheets or higher. High-thread-count claims may be inflated, or the sheets may have been manufactured with thinner, lower-quality threads. Sheets made from Egyptian cotton or American-grown pima are the best, regardless of thread count. They have the longest fibers, which means they'll last the longest.

Save $$: Up to $100 per sheet set depending on brand and size.

Save the Planet: Longer-lasting sheets, by definition, need to be replaced less frequently. Growing cotton requires energy, water, land, and large quantities of agrochemicals. Processing, sewing, and transport—most cotton items are made overseas—involve additional energy and resources.

Good for You: If you're not buying super-expensive sheets, you're staying away from luxury-linen departments, which can be major money suckers.

Sleep Naturally

The SHIFT: Buy organic cotton sheets from a discount store instead of designer nonorganic sheets at a department store.

Save $$: Up to $50–$150.

Save the Planet: Organic cotton is produced without chemical fertilizers and without harmful pesticides and herbicides. Organic farmers use practices that maintain soil quality and prevent the pollution of water bodies and ecosystems. Buying an organic cotton sheet set saves about 1.5 pounds of agrochemicals from entering the environment—and your bedroom.

LAUNDRY ROOM

Run Cold

The SHIFT: Instead of setting your washing machine to wash and rinse with hot water, choose to wash and rinse in cold—or at least wash in warm and rinse in cold.

Save $$: $50 per year in water heating costs if you make the shift for three loads per week.

Save the Planet: Save upward of 25 therms of natural gas or nearly 500 kilowatt-hours, as 90% of the energy used for clothes washing goes to heating the water.

Good for You: Your clothes will look their best for much longer.

SWIFT SHIFT:
IT ALL COMES OUT IN THE WASH

When I had the opportunity to renovate parts of my house because of a flood, I replaced my electricity-guzzling old appliances with ENERGY STAR qualified ones. So far, the results have been amazing. I'm saving between $50 and $100 on my electricity and water bills every month and my new washer cleans my clothes in less time, with less detergent.

Donna, San Fernando Valley, CA
Business Owner
Married, Mother of Jason, 18; Jeremy, 15; Klara, 7; and Lorenzo, 5

Soap Down

The SHIFT: Don't use more soap than is recommended in your washer.

Save $$: Up to $50 per year just by using the recommended amount, as opposed to throwing in about 50% more for each wash.

Save the Planet: Save the resources used to make the detergent and container. Decrease waste and reduce the concentration of chemicals in your wastewater or septic system.

Good for You: Using too much soap can make it difficult for the rinse cycle to completely eliminate the suds, so you may find that you'll have less skin irritation once there's less detergent buildup on your clothing. And if you usually set your washer to run a double-rinse cycle, you can save water (and more money) by rinsing only once.

Full Time

The SHIFT: Do laundry only when you can fill the washer to capacity. Washing small loads uses nearly the same amount of energy and only slightly less water than washing large ones.

Save $$: Up to $40 per year on water and energy costs if, by combining small loads, you wash one less load per week. You'll also save almost $15 per year on laundry soap.

Save the Planet: Conserve 1,700 gallons of water and about 570 pounds of carbon dioxide.

Good for You: Eliminating 52 loads a year will save you serious time. Consider that it takes about 2.5 minutes to load and unload the washer—more than two hours per year you could spend on more productive, enjoyable, or relaxing activities.

Throw Me a Line

The SHIFT: Try line-drying two loads of laundry (or more) per week.

Save $$: Up to $45 in energy costs per year.

Save the Planet: Save 425 kilowatt-hours of energy per year and more than 650 pounds of carbon dioxide.

Good for You: Clothes that are line-dried last longer than those that are dried in a dryer. After all, the lint that's collected in your dryer's lint trap is made of fibers pulled from your clothes. If you have nowhere to line-dry outside, try drying clothes inside on hangers or on a fold-up clothes rack.

UNSTAIN

Americans throw away a total of 1.4 billion pounds of shoes and clothing every year. If we all did a little more stain treating, this number could plummet.

Here's how:

- Treat the stain as soon as possible to prevent it from setting.
- Don't put a stained garment in the dryer until you've treated the stain. The dryer's heat will cause the stain to set.

For stains caused by . . .

- Berries, fruit, or juice: Pour boiling water on the stain. Pretreat if necessary and wash as usual.
- Grease, oil, or butter: Pour cornmeal or flour on the stain and let it sit and absorb the oil. Pretreat and wash as usual.
- Dirt and mud: Rub the cut end of a potato on the stain and let it set for a few hours before washing as usual.
- Grass stains: Rub out with white vinegar. Wash as usual.
- Wine: Soak in milk overnight—or rub on white toothpaste—then wash as usual. White wine can also be used to treat red wine stains.
- Almost any food-related stain can be removed with spit. Yes, spit. And sometimes it takes a lot to get the job done. The enzymes in your saliva are just as good as a stain stick, and they're free.

Sheets to the Wind

The SHIFT: Eliminate the use of conventional store-bought dryer sheets.

Save $$: Up to $40 per year on dryer sheet costs.

Save the Planet: Conserve the resources used to make the dryer sheets, as well as the waste they create when they're disposed of.

Good for You: Dryer sheets are filled with toxic chemicals, some of which are known carcinogens—did you know dryer sheets can be used to repel ants?

Shift-it Tip: Instead of using dryer sheets, pour a half cup of white vinegar in the washer to soften fabric, or place a couple of drops of essential oil on a piece of cloth and put it in the dryer with your clothes. Another option? Fill a small sealable canvas bag with dried herbs or natural potpourri—lavender smells great—and toss in with wet laundry, or choose reusable dryer sachets found at your local health-food store.

Screen Star

The SHIFT: Clean your dryer's lint screen before loading.

Save $$: Up to $35 per year in energy costs.

Save the Planet: Unclogging your lint screen increases your dryer's efficiency, which means your clothes take less time to dry and you use about 250 kilowatt-hours' less energy.

Good for You: Lint buildup can actually pose a fire danger. Can you imagine how embarrassing it would be if your house burned down just because you hadn't cleaned your lint trap?

SWIFT SHIFT: NOBODY'S PERFECT

Since we started shifting, we've learned to take pride in finding secondhand or "delicately used" items. Our washing machine clunked out recently, and instead of getting a new one, we bought a front-loader with a bigger load capacity at a scratch-and-dent warehouse. So we got a much better, more energy-efficient model for about $400 less than if we had bought it in perfect condition, brand-new. This will not only come in handy when we're washing baby clothes—yes, we know we need to run only full loads!—but will also save us an extra $50 per year in energy and water costs.

Jill and Jeremy, Orlando, FL
Medical Administrator and Realtor
Pet Lovers and Parents-to-Be

Makes Sensor

The SHIFT: Use the moisture sensor or "less dry" feature on your dryer instead of using the timed-dry setting.

Save $$: Up to $20 per year.

Save the Planet: Use up to 15% less energy compared with the timed-dry setting.

Good for You: Overdrying your clothes encourages static-cling buildup. So choosing the moisture sensor and using the "less dry" setting may actually reduce the static in your clothes. Exposing fibers to heat for less time will also help clothes last longer.

LANDSCAPE AND GARDENING

How Dry I Am

The SHIFT: If you live in a dry climate, consider replacing some portion of your lawn with drought-tolerant plants that are native to your region.

Save $$: Up to $80 per year on water expenses if your 5,000-square-foot irrigated lawn area is cut by half.

Save the Planet: Reduce water use by 40,000 gallons per year.

Good for You: Less grass means less mowing, which means you'll be saving either upward of 50 hours per year or the money you'd normally spend on a gardener. People with allergies will also suffer less if the grass is shorn less frequently.

Nature Made

The SHIFT: Use organic or natural fertilizer instead of synthetic or chemical fertilizer.

Even $$: Prices can be comparable.

Save the Planet: Natural and organic fertilizers are made from composted or dehydrated plant and animal materials, whereas synthetic fertilizers require tremendous amounts of fossil fuel energy to produce.

Good for You: Organic fertilizers don't create the health or environmental hazards that are associated with chemical fertilizers.

Made in the Shade

The SHIFT: Plant fast-growing shade trees on the east- and west-facing sides of your home.

Save $$: Up to $110 per year on air-conditioning bills.

Save the Planet: Save up to 1,055 kilowatt-hours' worth of electricity per year. Trees also provide habitat for birds and other wildlife.

Good for You: Trees can improve the aesthetics of a property, which can in turn enhance its value.

Incredible Edibles

The SHIFT: Plant an organic fruit and vegetable garden in your backyard.

Save $$: Up to $800 per year.

Save the Planet: Reduce environmental damage caused by conventional farming methods, which use large tractors, chemical fertilizers, and toxic pesticides. Also save energy on food transport.

Shift-it Tip: Almost anyone can cultivate a healthy garden—the key is not to overthink things. Visit http://shiftyourhabit.com for a step-by-step list of everything you'll need to know to be grocery shopping in your backyard in no time.

SWIFT SHIFT: GARDEN OF EATIN'

For me, planting our edible garden was more about returning to my roots than adopting an unfamiliar lifestyle. As the son of a preacher and grandson of a coal miner, I grew up growing vegetables and raising chickens and eggs. With everything available to us on the family farm, we didn't need to buy much back then. Now that my own family has a garden, we don't either. We've cut our food bills by about $800 this year.

Michael, Huntsville, AL
Biomedical Technician
Married, Father of Zoë, 12; Jackson, 5; and Cole, 4

What Your Edible Garden Can Save You

If the task of establishing a patch of delicious produce seems daunting, consider this: For every $1 you put toward your edible garden (including bags of compost, soil, pots, water, organic fertilizers, cages, netting, seeds, seedlings, etc.), you'll get an average of $9 back in produce.

Product	When to Plant	Time Until Harvest	Plot Size
Arugula	Spring	40 days	5 sq. ft.
Basil	Late spring	40 days	5 sq. ft.
Beets	Spring	60 days	5 sq. ft.
Bell pepper	Spring	75 days	10 sq. ft.
Butternut squash	Spring	90 days	5 sq. ft.
Chard	Early spring	60 days	10 sq. ft.
Green beans	Late spring	55 days	15 sq. ft.
Spinach	Spring and early fall	40 days	10 sq. ft.
Strawberries	Late spring	1 year	45 sq. ft.
Tomatoes	Spring	80 days	15 sq. ft.
Turnips	Spring and fall	50 days	5 sq. ft.
Yellow squash	Late spring	50 days	10 sq. ft.
Zucchini	Late spring	60 days	10 sq. ft.
TOTAL			150 sq. ft.

If you don't have the space in which to plant your own *potager*, join a community garden, where you can grow your own seasonal produce for next to nothing and strengthen your neighborhood's sense of community. Check out www.communitygarden.org to find the one closest to you. Purchasing a share in an organic CSA is also an affordable option that benefits farmers.

Number of Plants or Seeds*	Estimated Initial Cost	Average Yield	Estimated Value of Yield
50 seeds	$1.00	10 lbs.	$40.00
10 seeds 4 plants	$0.50 $4.00	4 lbs.	$20.00
80 seeds	$2.00	40 beets	$40.00
4 plants	$3.00 + cages	20 lbs.	$40.00
3 seeds	$0.50	10 squashes	$20.00
60 seeds	$1.50	25 lbs.	$50.00
40 seeds	$0.50	10 lbs.	$20.00
120 seeds	$2.00	30 lbs.	$90.00
25 plants	$10.00	25 pints	$50.00
4 plants	$3.00 + cages	100 lbs.	$320.00
80 seeds	$2.00	40 bulbs	$20.00
3 plants	$3.00	20 lbs	$40.00
3 plants	$3.00	25 lbs	$50.00
	$36.00		$800.00

*Starting your garden with seeds requires some thinning once the plants begin to grow, so you'll always plant more seeds than you would already-established plants.

LAWN CARE and IRRIGATION

Drip It Good

The SHIFT: Use drip irrigation or soaker hoses for flower beds instead of sprinklers.

Save $$: Up to $15 per year on water bills.

Save the Planet: Drip irrigation reduces the amount of water lost to evaporation, allowing you to reduce water use by 30% to 70%—an average of up to 8,100 gallons per year for 1,000 square feet of garden space—compared with standard sprinklers.

> **WATERMARKS**
>
> One-third of the water consumed by the average household is used outdoors, more than half to irrigate lawns and gardens. All together, Americans use more than 7 billion gallons of water per day for landscape irrigation.

Don't Overdo It

The SHIFT: Most lawns need only 1 inch of water per week to stay healthy.

Save $$: Up to $80 per year for a 2,500-square-foot lawn if you apply 1 inch of water instead of 2 inches.

Save the Planet: Conserve up to 40,000 gallons of water. Overwatering not only wastes water, but increases runoff, which sends fertilizers and other chemicals into sensitive water bodies and environments.

Good for You: An overwatered lawn can result in the emergence of fungus and disease, not to mention ruined high heels and muddy carpets.

Long and Strong

The SHIFT: Clip your lawn no shorter than 2 inches high.

Save $$: Up to $60 per year on water costs and an additional

$10–$20 or more on chemicals to fight pests and weeds for a 2,500-square-foot lawn.

Save the Planet: Cut your watering needs in half—possibly by as much as 30,000 gallons or more—and reduce the need for one fertilizer application per year.

Good for You: Keeping your grass a bit longer reduces stress, making it less vulnerable to weeds, insects, and disease. It also allows your lawn to dedicate energy to growing roots as opposed to growing foliage. You'll actually mow a longer lawn less frequently than a shorter one, which saves time.

A Good Clip

The SHIFT: Instead of collecting your grass clippings as you mow your lawn, leave them on the grass. They'll help your lawn retain moisture, and as they decompose they'll add nutrients to the soil.

Save $$: Up to $35 in water and fertilizer costs for a 2,500-square-foot lawn.

Save the Planet: Reduce the need for watering and save up to 9,000 gallons per year. By reducing the need for commercial fertilizers, you'll keep these chemicals from leaching into water supplies. Fertilizers are the most overused lawn product.

Good for You: Eliminate the time it takes to empty the grass catcher, which over the course of a year of mowing could total 150 minutes or more. Also save time buying and applying fertilizer.

Before Sunrise

The SHIFT: Set your sprinkler timers to water the lawn before sunrise as opposed to during the late morning, midday, or afternoon.

Save $$: Up to $20 on water costs per year for a 2,500-square-foot lawn.

Save the Planet: Evaporation is highest when the sun is up. Watering before dawn means you can set your sprinklers to run on shorter cycles, conserving roughly 20% to 25% of the water you'd otherwise lose to evaporation by watering during the day. An average household that currently waters during daylight hours could save up to 13,000 gallons per year by making this shift.

Clean Sweep

The SHIFT: Sweep sidewalks and driveways instead of hosing them down.

Save $$: Up to $10 per year on water costs.

Save the Planet: Conserve up to 5,000 gallons of water per year, depending on how long and how often you use the hose to clean the area around your property. You'll also keep contaminated runoff from entering storm drains, which may eventually flow into water bodies that form ecosystems.

Don't Get Hosed

The SHIFT: Buy an automatic shutoff nozzle for your hose instead of a continuous sprayer.

Save $$: Up to $5 per year in water costs if an automatic shutoff nozzle can reduce hose use by seven minutes per week.

Save the Planet: Letting the water run when you're not using it can waste up to 2,400 gallons of water per year or more.

POOL and OUTDOOR LIVING

Get It Covered

The SHIFT: Buy a swimming pool cover instead of using your pool heater.

Save $$: $535 per year or more on energy and water costs.

Save the Planet: Compared with an uncovered pool, a covered pool can save as much as 5,000 kilowatt-hours—more energy than the average home air conditioner uses annually. And, because of reduced evaporation, a covered pool can save more water than the average household uses in a week.

Good for You: Pool covers allow for the absorption of heat from the sun, creating a more comfortable temperature for swimming without the use of a pool heater. They also help keep out dirt and leaves.

Sensor-Ship

The SHIFT: Buy motion-sensor outdoor security or porch lighting instead of nonsensor lighting that runs throughout the night.

Save $$: Up to $160 on electricity bills per year.

Save the Planet: Conserve 500 kilowatt-hours of electricity per year.

Good for You: Deters trespassers!

Natural Lighting

The SHIFT: Choose solar lighting for outdoor gardens and walkways instead of standard electric accent lighting.

Save $$: Up to $25 on electric bills per year after initial cost difference. (Solar lighting costs about $5 more per lamp.)

Save the Planet: Conserve up to 210 kilowatt-hours of electricity— more than the indoor lighting energy used by the average household in over two and a half months.

Turn on the Gas

The SHIFT: Grill with a natural gas or an electric grill instead of a charcoal grill.

Save $$: $20–$30 per year on charcoal and lighter fluid costs.

Save the Planet: Unlike charcoal grills, gas and propane grills do not emit volatile organic compounds, nitrous oxide, or other toxins.

Good for You: Gas and propane grills cook food more evenly than charcoal ones and make the barbecuing process more time efficient.

HOME and GARDEN: The Bottom Line

The shifts listed in this chapter could save a household of four up to **$5,600** per year.

For more home ideas and to share your own experiences with making natural cleaning products and picking home-grown tomatoes, visit **http://shiftyourhabit.com.**

Monica, Jeremy, and William

Monica is a beauty professional living in Ventura County. Her husband, Jeremy, is a chef, and they have a son William, age six. Since Monica spends most of her time running from client to client, she needs solutions that enable her to give her family the highest quality of life with minimum effort.

When Elizabeth asked me whether we'd be interested in participating in Shift Your Habit, I couldn't really imagine what we needed help with. While we're not a family of environmental activists, we do try to recycle, we don't use plastic, we buy whatever we can preowned, and we attempt to live as organically as possible. I knew we could work on our gas budget—I drive a big, old truck—but I couldn't really figure out a way to improve my fuel efficiency. Since we couldn't afford to buy a new car, I told her thanks, but no thanks.

Then Elizabeth asked about food. I suspected there was a financial leak in our family, and it had dawned on me that it might be related to food waste. I've always been a bit neurotic about food and nutrition. I shopped every day to be sure things were fresh. I never ate, or fed my family, things that had been frozen. I threw away leftovers. I bought way too much of everything.

When I took the time to calculate our weekly grocery expenditures, I was shocked. I knew that the key to living less wastefully in the kitchen would be information. So that's when I agreed to be part of Shift Your Habit. I'm so glad I did.

My husband Jeremy, however, was very open-minded from the beginning. He started getting involved in how much we were spending at the grocery store, and on what. He knew we had to stop the financial leak as his fourteen-year-old car was on its last lap and would soon need to be replaced. Well, believe it or not, the food shifts we've made have saved us so much money that we were able to buy him that new car. If, a few months ago, you'd told me I could trade garbage bags full of food for a new car, I would have said you were crazy. Now, I'm living by a new motto: If I'm not going to use it, I don't buy it. And if I do buy it, I use it!

Monica, Ventura County, CA
Beauty Professional
Married, Mother of William, 6

FOOD and DRINK

My philosophy about food is pretty basic: Eat simple, wholesome ingredients combined in delicious ways that provide me and my son, Emmett, with calories rich in flavor and nutrition. I love picking vegetables from my home garden. I also like locally raised produce and grass-fed beef—yes, I eat meat!—and organic, hormone-free dairy products. I like foods with little-to-no packaging, no preservatives, and lots of taste. And guess what? It's not so expensive to eat this way. I know it might be easier (and sometimes less pricey) to zip in and out of a drive-thru than to get up five minutes earlier to make a sandwich. But putting in a few minutes is worth it when you consider the benefits of eating healthful, homemade recipes.

It's also important to remember that nourishment from meals isn't purely physical. Epicurus, the ancient Greek philospher, said, "We should look for someone to eat and drink with, before looking for something to eat and drink." He's right. Probably even more important than what we choose to eat is how we choose to eat it. Ideally, a meal should be enjoyed at the dinner table with friends and family, instead of gulped down in front of the television.

Sharing a meal is a way to connect, to nourish our bodies, our minds, and our relationships. And research shows that kids who eat dinner with their parents regularly are more likely to do well in school and less likely to have behavioral problems. I realize not every family can make this happen, but we should all strive to eat consciously—to make good choices when possible, eat together when possible, and give our food and mealtimes the attention they deserve.

Here's a bounty of good-eating tips to savor.

GROCERY SHOPPING

Unbrand

The SHIFT: Buy natural and organic store-brand basics instead of name-brand products.

Save $$: Consider the example below from a New York City store, which sells both brand-name products and private labels for natural and organic foods.

Save the Planet: Name-brand staples that are not organic contain pesticide residues and are highly processed, sometimes sacrificing nutrition.

Good for You: The more you can eliminate artificial ingredients and pesticide-laden products from your diet, the better.

Food	Price for Brand Name	Price for Store-Brand Natural
Sliced Swiss cheese	$9.18 for 12 oz.	$7.00 for 12 oz.
Strawberry frozen yogurt	$3.99 for 14 oz.	$3.99 for 1 pint
Tomato and basil pasta sauce	$3.49 for 26 oz.	$2.59 for 28 oz.
All-purpose flour	$2.29 for 2 lbs.	$1.79 for 2 lbs.
Puffed rice cereal	$4.99 for 12 oz.	$3.99 for 12 oz.
Trail mix	$7.38 for 12 servings	$6.49 for 12 servings
Total Spent	$31.32	$25.25

Bulk Up

The SHIFT: Buy food packaged in bulk instead of individually wrapped single-serving packages.

Save $$: Up to $500 per year.

Save the Planet: Keep an estimated 500 pounds' worth of packaging waste out of the landfill and conserve the resources to make that packaging and the energy used to transport it.

Shift-it Tip: Buying 100-calorie packs of cookies, crackers, and chips is a popular way to control portion size, but, according to the Center for Science in the Public Interest, they cost twice as much as family-size packages.

SWIFT SHIFT: SUPERMARKET SUPERSTARS

We were really excited to hit the grocery store after Elizabeth challenged us to improve our eating and food-buying habits. Grocery shopping was a totally new experience! Instead of individually packaged, processed foods, we chose bulk packs of whole foods. Instead of prepacked lunch kits, my girls bought the components to make their own. We switched regular produce for organic and eliminated the junk food that always draws us in when we're waiting in line at the register—simply by making a list.

Even though some of the organic stuff we bought was more expensive than what we usually buy, we cut out so many impulse purchases that we actually saved money. I never realized it before, but all the little incidentals are where the extra cost—and waste—really comes into play.

Samantha, Orange County, CA
Insurance Company Project Manager
Married, Mother of Allison, 15, and Kellie, 9

Winning Season

The SHIFT: Buy seasonal produce.

Save $$: Up to $130 or more per year if one-third of the produce you currently buy is out of season.

Save the Planet: Buying local, seasonal produce reduces the amount of transport energy—aka food miles—it takes to bring your food from farm to table. In order to carry certain fruits and vegetables year-round, supermarkets buy them from countries in the Southern Hemisphere. To preserve freshness and prevent bruising, growers package imported produce in excessive amounts of plastic and cardboard. Check the Country of Origin Label (COOL) produce sticker to see where an item originated.

Good for You: In order for out-of-season fruits and vegetables to survive their long-distance journey, it's necessary to harvest them long before they reach full ripeness. This may result in inferior taste, quality, and nutritional value compared with in-season produce.

WHERE DOES YOUR MONEY GO?

For every dollar you spend on processed food, only 19 cents goes to the farmers who grew the raw ingredients. The rest pays for things related to the marketing of the final product: 8 cents for packaging, 7.5 cents for transportation and energy, and about 40 cents for labor costs and markups by different links in the supply chain.

Shift-it Tip: Check out farmers' markets and farm stands for the best prices on truly local, seasonal produce. The U.S. Department of Agriculture's website (http://apps.ams.usda.gov/FarmersMarkets) has a handy search tool that will help you find farmers' markets in your area.

SWIFT SHIFT:
OUT OF THE TRASH AND ONTO THE TABLE

Because Monica had no idea how to store food properly, she threw her hands up—and threw everything away. Here were the questions she wanted to have answered before she agreed to shift her food habits.

Does storing fruits and vegetables lead to loss of nutrients?

Relatively little nutrient loss happens once the produce reaches your countertop or refrigerator. In general, food quality will not decrease significantly during storage as long as the food is stored properly and used within the recommended time frame.

How do I know what the shelf life is of certain foods?

The shelf life represents the time after which the product has lost some of its original quality and has nothing to do with the safety of eating "expired" produce. If there's any question, it doesn't hurt to use your senses (sight, smell, touch, taste) to determine whether a particular fruit or vegetable is edible or not. In many cases you can still eat something within a couple of days of its suggested use-by date. (Visit http://shiftyourhabit.com for more information on the storage and shelf life of specific foods.)

How can I ensure that my leftovers are safe to eat?

1. All leftovers should be refrigerated or frozen within two hours.
2. Label leftovers with the date.
3. Refrigerate and eat or freeze leftovers within 3 to 4 days.
4. Thaw frozen foods in the refrigerator or in the microwave on low power. Frozen food should not be thawed on the kitchen counter.

5. Reheat leftovers on the stovetop or in the microwave on glass or ceramic plates. Never microwave food in plastic containers.

I believe good nutrition is key to a child's development. And since I had always feared that food lost its nutrients once it was cooked or frozen, I'd been afraid to give my son frozen food or reheated leftovers. I was also concerned about storing and heating food in plastic, which I thought was my only option until Elizabeth turned me on to a set of glass storage containers with lids. Armed with a battery of information on food safety, I felt comfortable to begin shifting my habits. I started shopping less frequently. I learned to look inside my refrigerator and plan meals based on what I already had in the house. It was a moment of triumph when I realized that I had gone three days without stepping foot in the grocery store, and I was still serving healthy meals to my family.

Monica, Ventura County, CA
Beauty Professional, Married, Mother of William, 6

It All Comes Out in the Wash

The SHIFT: Don't bother buying commercial produce spray washes to clean your fruits and vegetables. Research shows that they are no more effective at cleaning your produce than cold running water and a vegetable brush.

Save $$: Up to $25 annually if you typically buy four bottles of produce wash per year.

Save the Planet: Save the energy and resources used to manufacture, transport, and dispose of the plastic spray bottle and its chemical contents.

Pot of Gold

The SHIFT: Instead of buying herbs at the grocery store, grow them in pots on a windowsill, porch, balcony, or flower bed. Popular herbs such as basil, oregano, mint, and rosemary are easy to grow.

Save $$: Up to $50 per year on fresh herbs if you currently buy a package every other week.

Save the Planet: Reduce the energy costs of transporting herbs from gardens to supermarkets, as well as the waste of the plastic packaging they're sold in.

Good for You: Growing your own herbs means you can snip just as much as you need for a particular dish as opposed to buying too much and having it spoil.

Can Ban

The SHIFT: Eat fresh fruits and vegetables instead of canned ones.

Save $$: The average U.S. household of four buys about 450 pounds of canned fruits and vegetables per year (although some of this weight is the can itself and liquid the food is swimming in). If instead you purchased an equivalent amount of fresh seasonal fruits and veggies, you could save $225 per year or more.

Save the Planet: The growing, processing, packaging, and transport of canned goods consume many times more energy than the production of fresh varieties.

Good for You: Fresh produce tends to have better flavor and is more versatile when it comes to preparing meals. Try to buy canned products only for long-term or emergency storage.

Shift-it Tip: If you can't find fresh varieties of the produce you're looking for, check out the freezer section. Frozen fruits and vegetables have more flavor and nutrition than canned ones.

BPA: NOT JUST IN WATER BOTTLES

Few people realize that most tin cans are lined with a white epoxy made from bisphenol A (BPA). BPA is a chemical that mimics estrogen and has been linked to breast cancer, early-onset puberty in adolescent girls, increased aggressiveness in males, and other hormone and reproductive system abnormalities. According to the Environmental Working Group, studies show that one in ten servings of canned food contains unsafe levels of BPA. For infant formula, it's one in three. The biggest culprits are canned pasta (i.e., ravioli, spaghetti, etc.), canned soup, canned vegetables, and meal replacement drinks. As with most prepared foods, you're better-off making your own meals using fresh ingredients.

Baked Goods

The SHIFT: Buy a fresh loaf of bread instead of packaged bread from the bread aisle.

Even $$: Prices can be comparable.

Save the Planet: Unlike plastic-packaged bread loaves, bakery bread is never frozen, requires little transport, and is usually wrapped in a recyclable paper bag. Bread-aisle bread requires nearly twice as much energy to produce as bakery bread.

Good for You: Bakery bread is freshly made, more flavorful, and less likely to contain preservatives than packaged bread.

Shift-it Tip: To keep bread fresher longer, store it at room temperature or frozen but never in the refrigerator.

Playing Ketchup

The SHIFT: Buy condiments in glass jars or bottles instead of plastic containers or squeeze bottles.

Even $$: Prices can be comparable.

Save the Planet: Glass is made from a nearly inexhaustible resource—sand—and is 100% recyclable into new glass containers. Plastic is made from petroleum. Because it loses its quality when broken down for recycling, plastic is almost never reincarnated into another food container.

SWIFT SHIFT: FULFILLING FILTER

We can't tell you how much we love our water filter and reusable water bottles. It feels so good to be able to pass by the beverage aisle at the market where we would usually buy water by the case. We ran the numbers and we're saving nearly $900 per year just by shifting our bottled water habit. We're also keeping about 70 pounds of plastic out of the landfill.

Jill and Jeremy, Orlando, FL
Medical Administrator and Realtor
Pet Lovers and Parents-to-Be

Free Refills

The SHIFT: Use a faucet or pitcher filter and a refillable water bottle or canteen instead of buying disposable plastic water bottles.

Save $$: Up to $500 per year if you spend an average of $10 per week on bottled water.

Save the Planet: Conserve fossil fuels—plastic is a petroleum product, after all—as well as about 30 pounds of plastic waste per year. Even when plastic bottles are recycled, they aren't recycled into new plastic bottles. They undergo an effect called *downcycling*, which means they lose their quality in the recycling process. As a result, they're good only for things like filler for fleece coats, parking lot bumpers, or fake wood for patio furniture.

Good for You: While the Environmental Protection Agency regularly tests regional tap water, it does not do the same for bottled water. In fact, past studies have found some bottled water to contain high levels of contamination, including arsenic, synthetic chemicals, and potentially harmful bacteria.

Shift-it Tip: When shopping for a reusable water bottle, opt for aluminum, stainless steel, or glass instead of hard plastic. Many hard plastics contain bisphenol A, which has been shown to have a negative impact on reproductive health, especially for children (see page 73).

Cola Cutback

The SHIFT: Reduce your soda consumption.

Save $$: Up to $650 per year by reducing soda purchases by just two 12-packs per week.

Save the Planet: Save the energy and resources used to make the soft drinks, manufacture the cans or bottles, and transport the finished product to your local market. Also reduce can and bottle waste and the energy it takes to transport the materials to either a recycling facility or a landfill.

Good for You: If the phosphoric acid in a can of cola is strong enough to clean the rust off a corroded car battery, what's it doing to your belly?

CARBONATION

Soft drinks are Americans' most-consumed beverages, followed by, in descending order, bottled water, coffee, fruit drinks and juices, beer, milk, tea, wine, spirits, and finally, vegetable juice. The average American drinks 50 gallons of soda per year.

Bubble Up

The SHIFT: Make your own soda. If you like the fizz but hate the hassle of buying bottle after bottle of sparkling water or soda, make it at home with a soda maker using carbon dioxide cartridges.

Save $$: After the initial purchase price, which ranges from $40 to $150, save $400 or more annually on soft drink purchases.

Save the Planet: Prevent the disposal of hundreds of cans and plastic bottles per year.

Good for You: No need to break your back carrying home cases of water bottles and soda cans. Making carbonated beverages yourself allows you to control the amount of fizz in your soft drink.

Shift-it Tip: Let your kids be the official carbonators. They'll get a kick out of the magical process and you can give them an impromptu chemistry lesson.

SWEET NOTHINGS

Drinking a can of regular soda means consuming as much as 11 teaspoons of sugar—that's as much as you'd get from eating six sugar cookies. Even worse, most sodas are sweetened with high-fructose corn syrup, which is associated with scores of health problems, including tooth decay, diabetes, obesity, a weakened immune system, and even heart problems.

Diet sodas come with their own issues. Even though they're noncaloric, they're chock-full of chemicals that can stimulate the appetite and impede the body's absorption of vitamins and minerals.

Phosphoric acid, which is found in both regular and diet sodas, has been associated with renal failure, kidney stones, osteoporosis, and impeding the absorption of calcium.

Do your family a favor and help them kick the soda habit.

Can It

The SHIFT: When you do buy soft drinks, choose aluminum cans instead of plastic bottles.

Save $$: Up to $1–$2 per 12-pack, or more than $200 per year if you buy two packs per week.

Save the Planet: Aluminum cans are superior to plastic bottles in terms of recyclability, the amount of recycled content they contain, and the energy needed to manufacture them. Aluminum cans contain an average of 40% recycled content, while the average plastic soda bottle contains less than 10% recycled content, if any at all. Plus, aluminum cans can be reincarnated into new aluminum cans indefinitely.

Good for You: If you're looking to reduce your soft drink consumption, buying the 6- or 12-ounce cans rather than 24-ounce plastic bottles may help you with portion control.

Great Grapes

The SHIFT: Buy value-priced organic wine (or wine made from organic grapes) from a startup vineyard instead of conventional wine from a more established one.

Save $$: Up to $10 or more per bottle, or over $500 per year if you buy one bottle of wine each week.

Save the Planet: Both organic wine and wine made from organic grapes are produced from vineyards managed without the use of chemical fertilizers and pesticides. This reduces soil, water, and air pollution in wine countries around the world.

Good for You: Avoid exposure to chemical residues, which can show up in wines made from conventionally grown grapes. There is also some evidence that people who normally get headaches from drinking wine feel no pain from organic wine because it's sulfite-free.

Shift-it Tip: Organic wine doesn't contain sulfites.

Home Brew

The SHIFT: If you have the time and patience, brew your own beer. Starter kits and home-brewing equipment are easy to come by. Save even more by buying beer gear secondhand.

Save $$: Up to $1,250 per year if you typically drink a six-pack of microbrew every week.

Save the Planet: Home brew is less energy intensive, uses less water, and produces less waste and greenhouse gas emissions than beer made in monstrous distilleries. And because the brewing occurs just steps away from your fridge, there are very few transport costs involved.

Good for You: By brewing at home, you can ensure that only the finest and purest ingredients are used.

Shift-it Tip: Bottles of home brew make great gifts, especially if you make homemade labels.

BOOZE BY THE NUMBERS

The United States ranks fortieth in the world in alcohol consumption per capita. Americans drink an average of more than 25 gallons of alcoholic beverages per year—about 2.25 gallons of pure alcohol per person. Per capita consumption in Luxembourg, ranked first, is twice as high. Ireland and Hungary are close behind.

Dilute It Yourself

The SHIFT: If you're going to drink juice made from concentrate, buy the frozen variety and add the water yourself instead of buying a prediluted carton in the refrigerator section.

Save $$: Up to $300 per year.

Save the Planet: A small frozen cardboard container produces less waste and costs less to transport than a plastic jug or a waxed paperboard carton.

Shift-it Tip: If you prefer ready-to-drink juices, try to find varieties labeled "not from concentrate."

Two for One

The SHIFT: If you're a milk lover, buy milk by the gallon instead of the half gallon.

Save $$: Up to $115 per year.

Save the Planet: A single large container requires less production energy and results in less waste than two small ones. Buying 1-gallon jugs of milk will reduce your waste production by about 12 pounds per year compared with buying twice as many half-gallon plastic jugs.

Shift-it Tip: Warn your kids that a gallon of milk is heavier than they think.

SWIFT SHIFT: CHANGE—IT'S IN THE BAG

At the beginning of this process, I had a hard time remembering to bring my reusable bags to the grocery store. But about two weeks into our shifts, my husband and I did a huge shopping trip. I remembered all my bags—and we filled them all! I remember walking out of the store with my shopping bags and being really proud of us. I know it sounds like a little thing, but considering we were bringing home about 420 shopping bags per year, this shift is going to keep a lot of plastic out of the landfill.

Samantha, Orange County, CA
Insurance Company Project Manager
Married, Mother of Allison, 15, and Kellie, 9

The Best Thing Since Sliced Cheese

The SHIFT: Buy block cheese instead of presliced or shredded cheese.

Save $$: Up to $100 per year for a family of four that buys 4 pounds of cheese per month.

Save the Planet: Block cheeses involve less processing and less plastic packaging than shredded or sliced cheeses, which results in less energy consumption and less waste.

Good for You: Block cheese gives you more versatility in how it can be used for snacks, appetizers, or meals.

What a Turkey

The SHIFT: Use ground turkey instead of ground beef.

Even $$: Prices can be comparable.

Save the Planet: Raising 1 pound of turkey or chicken requires 75% less energy from fossil fuels, 85% less water, and half the land required to produce 1 pound of beef. Poultry farms are also less polluting to air and water.

Good for You: Ground turkey breast has less saturated fat and less cholesterol than ground beef.

Shift-it Tip: If you think ground turkey tastes dry compared to beef because of its lower fat content, try mixing in some finely diced onions, carrots, and celery. This French technique will keep the meat juicy and flavorful.

SWIFT SHIFT: WASTE NOT, WANT NOT

We rarely, if ever, waste food. Just before something looks as though it's on the verge of going bad, we put it in the freezer. For example, when fruit starts getting too ripe, we freeze it to use in smoothies. We always keep sliced loaves of bread frozen to prevent them from getting stale or moldy. I guess if you figure we're actively preserving about $10 worth of food per week, this habit is saving us more than $500 per year.

Mary and Tom, Staten Island, NY
Retired Teacher and Communications Specialist

Extend the Life of Your Perishables

Think back to how many times you've thrown away stuff you really meant to eat. It's extremely guilt inducing, I know. But let go of the guilt and move on. Here are some ways to keep fresh things fresher, longer.

To prolong the life of ...	Just ...
Fresh fruits and vegetables	Soak in a bowl of water with 1 tablespoon of vinegar and a dash of salt.
Fruits with pits	Refrigerate with seed(s) intact.
Cookies	Place a crust of bread in a sealed bowl or jar with the cookies to keep them soft and fresh.
Spinach, lettuce, leafy greens	(1) Store in an airtight bowl of water in the refrigerator. OR (2) Rinse in cold water and shake off as much water as possible. Wrap in cheesecloth or paper towel to soak up the condensation that contributes to spoilage. Store in an airtight container.
Block cheese	Shred it and store it in the freezer. Frozen shredded cheese is perfect for lasagna, casseroles, nachos, and other gooey dishes.
Carrots with greens attached	Remove the greens as soon as you bring them home and store the carrots in an airtight container in the fridge.
A small piece of expensive cheese	(1) Wrap in aluminum foil. OR (2) Wrap in a paper towel dampened with white vinegar, then seal in plastic wrap or an airtight container.

Shift-it Tip: Produce purchased at the farmers' market generally lasts longer than produce purchased at the supermarket. This is because it spends less time off the vine in transport from the farm to your table.

Chicken Big

The SHIFT: Cook with whole chickens, not cut-up ones.

Save $$: Up to $600 per year if all chicken (4 pounds per week) is purchased whole instead of as boneless, skinless breasts.

Save the Planet: Reduce the energy, resources, and waste involved with processing, packaging, and transport.

SWIFT SHIFT: A REAL MEAL DEAL

We buy whole chickens because we can get three meals—or more—out of a single bird. On the first night, we cut it into pieces and make chicken soup by poaching it in water. We pull the breasts out of the pot after twenty minutes of simmering and use one to make a Waldorf salad and the other to make a chicken pot pie. After using some of the broth for soup, we freeze the rest in ice cube trays to use for gravy or broth in future meals.

Mary and Tom, Staten Island, NY
Retired Teacher and Communications Specialist

Meat Less

The SHIFT: Cut meat out of your diet one day per week and replace it with rice, potatoes, soy, or lentils.

Save $$: A family of four that reduces its meat consumption by just 2 pounds per week can save about $250 per year.

Save the Planet: Raising livestock consumes more energy, land, and water and produces more pollution and greenhouse gases than growing potatoes, soy, lentils, or rice.

Good for You: All else being equal, eating a diet with more whole grains and fiber-rich foods and less meat may reduce your risk of developing cardiovascular problems.

Shift-it Tip: Easily substitute tofu in any dish that calls for beef or chicken.

Ice Ice Baby

The SHIFT: Buy flash-frozen instead of fresh fish. Much of the fish available for sale these days is frozen at sea shortly after being caught. So this means most "fresh" fish was previously frozen anyway—just thawed for presentation.

Save $$: Prices vary by species, but frozen fish tends to cost less than fresh fish, mainly because its shelf life is longer and there's less spoilage at the seafood counter.

Save the Planet: Even though fish are renewable resources—meaning their populations can be replenished over time—more than 70% of fish species around the world are endangered. The more we can prevent spoilage and the wasting of fish, the closer we'll get to preserving threatened populations.

Shift-it Tip: When buying frozen fish, look for product that is either vacuum sealed or has a layer of ice on it. Flash-frozen fish is most likely to maintain its quality.

GOING FISHING

The most eco-friendly way to eat seafood is to be sure your choices are harvested sustainably and in a way that doesn't damage the surounding marine ecosystem or other species. To find out which fish are safe, just send a text message to FishPhone, a service of the Blue Ocean Institute, which will instantly send you sustainability info about a fish species. Just text the word *fish* and the name of the fish in question to 30644.

What's Worth It

Here's when it makes sense to spend a little more.

Label	What You'll Find It On	What It Means
USDA ORGANIC — USDA Organic Produce	Vegetables, fruits, grains, nuts, lentils	Grown without synthetic fertilizers or pesticides and with farming techniques that protect soil quality, minimize erosion, and actively prevent the contamination of air, land, and water.
USDA ORGANIC — USDA Organic Meats and Dairy	Milk, eggs, chicken, beef	Livestock are fed organic feed. Synthetic hormones, antibiotics, chemicals, and genetic engineering are prohibited. The living environment must be stress-free and promote the health and well-being of the animals, as well as prevent the contamination of air, land, and water.
Grass-Fed	Beef	Cattle are raised on pastures or are fed hay instead of corn feed, the farming of which requires enormous quantities of chemical fertilizers, pesticides, and diesel fuel (for transportation). Grass-fed cattle are not treated with antibiotics or hormones.
FAIR TRADE CERTIFIED — Fair Trade	Coffee, tea, chocolate	Poor farmers of these products in developing countries receive fair market prices, workers enjoy safe working conditions and fair wages, communities receive development assistance and investment in social programs, and crops are grown with sustainable farming methods and without the use of pesticides or genetically modified organisms.
Wild	Salmon	Wild salmon (aka Alaskan or Pacific salmon) is generally a sustainably caught fish. It's the best alternative to farmed salmon (aka Atlantic salmon), which is associated with major environmental problems in the marine environment. Wild salmon is also less likely to contain unhealthy levels of mercury, PCBs, hormones, antibiotics, or other contaminants, which are associated with some farmed salmon.

COOKING

The Micro Wave

The SHIFT: Cook in the microwave oven instead of in an electric oven.

Save $$: Up to $35 in energy costs per year (assuming you use it to cook four meals per week).

Save the Planet: Save enough energy to cook 950 microwaveable meals.

Good for You: Save 156 hours per year, as microwaves cook more efficiently than convection ovens—usually in about a quarter of the time or less.

Shift-it Tip: Keep your microwave clean. Splatters can affect efficiency and performance—as well as make new food taste off.

Contain Yourself

The SHIFT: Use microwave-safe glass or ceramic dishes. Never microwave food in plastic containers—even if they claim to be microwave safe.

Save $$: Up to $25 per year on plastic container replacements.

Save the Planet: Conserve the resources—mainly petroleum—used to make the plastics as well as the waste produced when they're disposed of.

Good for You: Research continues to show that plastics are prone to leaching potentially harmful chemicals into food. Even at doses that the U.S. Food and Drug Administration (FDA) and the plastics industry claim are harmless, there is evidence that cellular damage can occur, especially in infants and young children. The main culprit, bisphenol A, has been found to leach from all types of plastics and is associated with reproductive and developmental disorders.

Shift-it Tip: If you usually heat frozen dinners in the microwave, just open the package and pop the frozen contents onto a glass or ceramic plate or bowl. Cover it with another glass plate or lid and cook it for the time recommended on the box.

SWIFT SHIFT: FROM PICKY EATERS TO HEALTHY HARVESTERS

Elizabeth was convinced that my kids' picky eating habits could be shifted. I was skeptical. So she took us to the home of an organic chef with her own kitchen garden and the boys got the chance to harvest produce directly from the soil. It turned out that they loved picking these healthy greens so much that they didn't mind eating them! The chef then taught us how to make a bunch of easy dishes—such as beef fajitas and a Swiss chard frittata—that took very little time to prepare, packed a nutritious punch, and helped us repurpose the leftovers into entirely new meals. Months after trying them for the first time, my boys still ask for these dishes regularly. Now, instead of buying fast food or frozen dinners, I'm preparing meals ahead of time and repurposing leftovers into brand-new creations! I figure we're saving at least $15 per week—or $800 per year!—by shifting our family meal habits.

Melanie, Los Angeles, CA
Middle School Teacher
Married, Mother of Miles, 10, and David, 5

The Pressure Is On

The SHIFT: Use an electric pressure cooker instead of your stovetop or oven to cook meals.

Save $$: Up to $35 per year in energy costs if you use it instead of your electric range an average of three times per week.

Save the Planet: Roughly 165 kilowatt-hours of electricity per year.

Good for You: Pressure cookers take a fraction of the time—merely minutes—required to cook a meal on the stove or in an oven. Unlike those of a generation ago, today's models are designed with safety in mind. And rumor has it they can cook almost anything.

Boiling Point

The SHIFT: Use an electric teakettle, which is highly efficient at heating water, instead of a stovetop tea kettle, which results in lots of energy wasted as your burner heats the surrounding air in addition to your hot water.

Save $$: Up to $40 in energy costs per year for a household that heats water on the stovetop twice a day.

Save the Planet: Save 15 therms of natural gas or 455 kilowatt-hours of electricity, depending on your stove type.

Good for You: Electric teakettles can heat water in less than half the time of stovetop ones, allowing you to enjoy your warm beverage a few minutes sooner each morning. They're also easier to clean, and most have automatic shutoffs.

Oil Slick

The SHIFT: Reuse frying oil from one meal to the next.

Save $$: Up to $90 per year if you save one quart of the oil you use per week.

Save the Planet: Save oil from being dumped down the drain (which should never be done, by the way) as well as the waste of the plastic bottles.

Good for You: Truth be told, you're better-off oven-frying than deep-frying. Most recipes can be converted; just coat items in bread crumbs—Japanese panko works best—and slowly brown in a 350 degree F oven.

Scrap Medal

Whether it's lemon peel, bacon grease, or day-old coffee, why not find a way to make use of it?

What it is:	What to do with it:
Meat drippings	Freeze in ice cube trays as gravy base
Raw meat scraps, bones, and skin	Simmer to make soup base
Bacon grease	Use for sautéing
Citrus skin	Use zest in baking
Coffee	Make iced coffee drinks
Flat beer	Create a base for fondue
Flat soda	Make a tenderizing marinade
Bread	Toast into croutons, blitz into crumbs

A Good Fit

The SHIFT: Fit your pot or pan to your burner.

Save $$: Up to $40 per year if you cook every day.

Save the Planet: Using a small pot on a large burner can waste up to 40% of your cooking energy.

Cover Up

The SHIFT: You've heard the saying "A watched pot never boils." Why? Water boils much faster when pots are covered, which means cooking that rice or pasta will take less time and use less energy.

Save $$: Up to $5 or more per year on energy costs.

Save the Planet: Conserving this much energy reduces carbon dioxide emissions by more than 50 pounds per year.

Good for You: Boiling water with the lid on takes 20% less time than boiling water in an uncovered pot. If you make this shift every day, you'll save an estimated 18 hours per year of cooking time.

Shift-it Tip: When you're grilling outside, tempting as it is to repeatedly peek at the meat (or veggies) roasting on the barbie, it's important to keep a lid on it. Your food will cook 5 to 10 minutes faster and use less fuel, saving you up to $40 in propane costs per year.

Double Up

The SHIFT: When preparing certain dishes that can be easily reheated (e.g., soups, casseroles, rice and pasta dishes, etc.), try doubling the recipe and freezing leftovers for a future meal.

Save $$: Up to $10 per year on energy bills if you double a recipe once a week.

Save the Planet: Conserve the gas or electricity you'd normally use to cook or bake an extra meal per week if you reheat the leftovers in the microwave.

Good for You: Save up to 50 hours per year of kitchen prep time, cooking, and cleanup. Doubling a recipe takes significantly less time than making a single recipe on two separate days.

JUST FREEZE IT

So many of us are unsure about the rules when it comes to freezing fresh foods. We want them to be safe to eat and to taste fresh, not freezer burned. Here are some easy rules to live by:

- According to the U.S. Department of Agriculture (USDA), food kept at 0 degrees F will *always* be safe. If you store something for more than a few months, eating it won't kill you—but I can't vouch for its taste.

- Freezing something at its peak quality will keep it tasting fresher longer. If you make a big pot of soup or sauce and know your family won't eat all of it, freeze it as soon as it cools instead of waiting a couple of days while it ages in the fridge.

- If you buy meat in bulk, remove it from its supermarket packaging and wrap each piece individually in waxed paper or freezer paper. Then place it in a sealable bag, airtight container, or plastic wrap before freezing. This will prevent freezer burn and allow you to defrost only as much as you need, when you need it, cutting down on waste.

- For vegetables, cooked (or blanched) freeze better than raw.

- When it comes to main dishes, the wetter the better. Soups, stews, and sauces are ideal for freezer storage.

No Time Like the Present

The SHIFT: Unless you're baking a dish that needs to rise (like a bread product), you can usually just place your dish in the oven and turn it on. Your food will start cooking as soon as the oven begins heating up and will likely still finish in the time estimated by the recipe.

Save $$: Up to $10 per year on energy costs if you bake without reheating three times per week.

Save the Planet: Nearly 9 therms of natural gas—enough to bake an additional two batches of cookies every week of the year.

Shift-it Tip: Although there may be times when your oven needs to be preheated, your broiler never has to be preheated. So don't turn it on until your food is already in and ready to cook.

Take Five

The SHIFT: When baking, turn off your oven 5 to 10 minutes before your food is done. Cooking will continue in the hot oven, but you'll conserve energy.

Save $$: Up to $15 per year if you use the oven three times per week.

Save the Planet: Conserve natural gas energy and reduce greenhouse gas emissions by more than 100 pounds per year.

Good for You: Although your dish will keep cooking in the hot oven, it won't be quite the scalding temperature it was when the oven was on. So you may be able to eat your meal sooner, as the dish won't have to cool off as much when you remove it from the oven.

Put a Lid on It

The SHIFT: Use reusable containers to store food instead of plastic zipper bags.

Save $$: Up to $50 per year on plastic bag costs if you use one bag per day, on average.

Save the Planet: Reduce plastic bag waste as well as the resources to make the bags.

Good for You: You don't have to remember to put zipper bags on your shopping list.

Foiled Again

The SHIFT: Reduce your use of aluminum foil—it's rarely necessary. Don't wrap food in aluminum foil that can be placed in a reusable container, and don't line pans with foil when baking or broiling.

Save $$: Up to $20 per year if you cut your use of aluminum foil by an average of 1 foot a day.

Save the Planet: Aluminum production involves huge amounts of energy, mining waste, and water pollution.

One Man's Trash . . .

The SHIFT: Instead of tossing those melon rinds, orange peels, coffee grounds, and eggshells in the trash, create a designated kitchen container that can collect them. Then empty it into a compost bin or green-waste barrel.

Save $$: If you choose to compost, you can save yourself $20 per year or more on bagged potting soil and artificial fertilizers.

Save the Planet: Composting half of all of your food scraps would keep 300 pounds of garbage per year out of the landfill for the average household.

Good for You: Using compost to replenish the nutrients in your soil will allow you to grow plants and vegetables without the use of chemical fertilizers, which can be hazardous to human and animal health as well as to local waterways.

Shift-it Tip: Any type of plant or animal material is biodegradable and can theoretically be composted. However, the list of items accepted in green-waste bins varies by city. Check with your green-waste hauler for specifics.

Bringing Foods Back to Life

Instead of tossing food that you think is going bad, you may be able to revive and repurpose it. Keeping edible food out of the trash reduces not only waste but also the cost and energy used to transport that waste to a landfill. Here are some creative ways to revive the stuff you'd normally toss.

If you have . . .	Just . . .
Stale cereal, crackers, chips, or nuts	Bake them in a 300 degree F oven for 3 to 5 minutes. Place in an airtight container and use within a couple of days.
Overripe bananas	Mix them into banana bread or cookie batter, cooked oatmeal, pudding, or smoothies. In the future, when you have a banana surplus, peel and freeze before they go brown. You can even impale them on Popsicle sticks and pass them off to your kids as dessert. (A chocolate-dipped banana is a real treat.)
Wilted lettuce or leafy greens	Soak them in cold water for 30 minutes to revive freshness.
Bruised fruit	Cut off the bruised area and chop the rest into a fruit or green salad.
Slightly sour milk (not moldy milk)	Use it to make scones, corn bread, or another baked recipe that calls for milk. You can also use it to moisten pancake batter.
Dried-out dried fruit	Place it in a Pyrex bowl or jar and cover in boiling water.
Limp celery	Add it to a stir-fry, soup, or meat dish.
Crystallized sugar—brown or white	Microwave it for 30 seconds to soften.
Half-used jars of pasta sauce	Freeze it in ice cube trays and use in future culinary masterpieces.

Leftover Makeover

The SHIFT: Make new meals out of your leftovers.

Save $$: Up to $520 per year of repurposing leftovers can save you $10 per week on food costs.

Save the Planet: Reduce food waste. Just because it's decomposable doesn't mean it will decompose in a landfill.

Good for You: Bring the Thanksgiving sensibility to the rest of your life. Some things really do taste better the next day!

SWIFT SHIFT: HASTE MAKES WASTE

While for some, saving leftovers is second nature, for a surprising number of Americans leftovers are considered waste and automatically get tossed in the trash. In fact, the U.S. Department of Agriculture estimates that the average American family throws away 14% of its food—or almost $600 worth per year. It turns out Monica was wasting much, much more.

Because of our frequent shopping and no-leftovers policy, we were throwing away almost 40 pounds of food per week—almost $100 worth!—most of it still perfectly edible. Now that I'm more informed—and I've obtained a set of glass storage containers that are easy to work with—we refrigerate our extra food and really do eat it again. I admit that I still find dealing with left-over leftovers immensely annoying. And I'm still trying to accept the fact that nutritious foods will still have value once they come out of the freezer. But at least I'm trying.

Monica, Ventura County, CA
Beauty Professional
Married, Mother of William, 6

EATING OUT

Open a Nestaurant

The SHIFT: Stay in for dinner instead of going out.

Save $$: Up to $1,500 per year if you eat in for two additional dinners per month.

Save the Planet: There are environmental benefits related to lower energy and water consumption, as restaurants consume huge amounts of both. You'll also save fuel by not driving out to dinner as often. For an average restaurant distance of 5 miles, you'll save up to 11 gallons or more—a full tank over the course of a year.

Good for You: Enjoy the comfort of home, use local and organic ingredients, and create healthier recipes with the foods you like the most. You can also cultivate your inner chef by experimenting with new flavors, ingredients, and cooking styles.

> **OVERINDULGENCE?**
>
> The typical American eats 313 meals per year at restaurants—almost one for every day of the year—and the average household of four spends almost $4,050 on meals out annually, just slightly less than the $5,115 spent on meals at home.

Bar None

The SHIFT: Instead of meeting for drinks at a bar before dinner, have appetizers and a glass of wine or a cocktail at home before you go out.

Save $$: Up to $1,000 per year if you typically have a couple of drinks at the bar before dinner once a week. You'll save twice as much if snacking at home dissuades you from ordering an appetizer.

Save the Planet: To meet health and safety requirements, food and drink establishments use much more water and energy to wash used glasses than you do in your home.

Good for You: It's easier to control the amount you're drinking when you're the one doing the pouring.

Be Your Own Barista

The SHIFT: Brew your own coffee and tea instead of stopping by the local chain on your way to work. For a week's worth of café lattes, you could buy enough Fair-Trade Certified gourmet beans to make a month's worth of coffee.

Save $$: Up to $700 per year by drinking coffee shop lattes every other day instead of every day. See? I'm not even asking you to give them up entirely!

Save the Planet: Unless you bring your own mug to the coffee shop, those paper cups and plastic lids are likely being sent to the landfill. Making your own coffee means reducing waste and saving resources.

Shift-it Tip: If you can't give up your café-made morning fix, at least bring your own cup.

SWIFT SHIFT: EATING IN

Another thing Elizabeth opened our eyes to was how much we were spending by eating out. What my husband, Jeremy, cooks is much better than what we could get at a restaurant anyway. So now I think about eating out like making a trade-off: We can save up for things we need—like a new computer for William—or we can spend money at a restaurant. When you look at it like that, it's not a very hard choice to make.

Monica, Ventura County, CA
Beauty Professional, Married, Mother of William, 6

You've Got It Made

Restaurant meals cost, on average, between three and six times more than those eaten at home. Are they really exponentially more delicious?

Who knows, but they're definitely more caloric, with an average of 85% more calories than the average home-cooked meal—and restaurant leftovers are more likely to get wasted.

Compare the cost of making these meals at home with eating them at a restaurant.

Meal	Homemade Cost Per Person	Typical Restaurant Cost Per Person	Savings by Cooking at Home for a Family of Four
Oatmeal with raisins plus coffee or orange juice	$0.50	$7.00 + tax + tip	$30.00
Swiss chard and cheese fritatta plus iced tea or lemonade	$1.25	$10.00 + tax + tip	$40.00
Pasta with tomatoes and basil plus glass of wine or soft drink	$2.50	$16.00 + tax + tip	$70.00
Roasted chicken with vegetables plus beverage	$3.25	$14.00 + tax + tip	$60.00
Grilled chicken salad plus iced tea or soft drink	$3.50	$13.00 + tax + tip	$50.00
Steak fajitas with poblano chiles and black beans plus beverage	$3.50	$17.00 + tax + tip	$70.00

MAKE THE MOST OUT OF YOUR MEAL OUT

Going out to eat should be something special. What's more frustrating than spending a day's pay on a slimy, underwhelming salad?

Here's how to really get what you pay for:

Contain yourself. Bring your own to-go container to portion-out your leftovers even before you start eating.

Go halfsies. Share an entree with your date.

Vegetate. Go meatless once in a while.

Get tapped. Say no to bottled water.

Eat on the walk. Find a place nearby and leave your car at home.

Break the chain. Support your local mom-and-pop spot.

Smoothie Operator

The SHIFT: Make your own smoothies by blending some frozen fruit with a splash of juice, milk, or soy milk.

Save $$: Up to $100 per year if, once a week, you make your own smoothie instead of buying one.

Save the Planet: Keep hundreds of 24-ounce Styrofoam cups and plastic lids out of landfills. Most municipalities don't recycle foam because it tends to be more costly than recycling other forms of plastic. If you still opt to visit the smoothie shop, bring your own reusable 24-ounce cup. You might even get a discount!

Good for You: Making your own smoothies means you control what goes into them. So you can choose organic ingredients and sugar-free juices. You can also experiment with various combinations of fruits to create your own signature drink.

SWIFT SHIFT: TWO-FER

We have always gone halfsies in restaurants, boxing up a portion of our entrees for another meal. Compared with eating our whole meal in one sitting—or tossing half in the trash—this habit is saving us $500 per year—not to mention tens of thousands of calories. As you age, you have to be careful to decrease your food intake, or else you end up growing as big as a house. And you'll be amazed at how much more filling a meal is when you eat it slowly.

Mary and Tom, Staten Island, NY
Retired Teacher and Communications Specialist

FOOD AND DRINK:
The Bottom Line

The shifts listed in this chapter could save the average family up to $9,100 or more.

For more culinary inspiration, and to share your own experiences with making your own soda, repurposing leftovers, and cooking vegetarian, check out http://shiftyourhabit.com.

MEET THE SHIFTERS:
Melanie, Al, Miles, and David

Melanie teaches at an urban middle school in Los Angeles, and makes extra income by redesigning and selling used clothing. Her husband, Al, runs his own screen-printing company. Melanie and Al want to help their energetic and athletic boys, Miles, age ten, and David, age five, establish healthy habits now that will pay off over the course of their lifetimes.

I've always been conscious about how I spend money. With two growing boys, we don't have extra money to waste. If I'm going to buy green products, for example, I need to be sure that they'll really work. In the same way, while I want to serve my family healthy food, my husband and I both work and we need to be able to put meals together quickly. Add that to the fact that my boys are really picky eaters and aren't going to willingly exchange chicken nuggets and french fries for a plateful of vegetables. Believe me, the last thing you want to do after spending a day with a classroom full of preteens is fight with your kids about what's for dinner.

So I suppose, more than anything, I was a bit leery of the shifts Elizabeth would recommend to us. I thought they wouldn't fit our lifestyle. They'd be too expensive, too time-consuming, not tasty enough, or just totally weird. Boy, was I wrong.

Of course there have been bumps along the way, but mostly the shifts we've made have been surprisingly easy, and they have changed our lives for the better. This process has impacted us both financially and in terms of our conscience. We feel very proud that we are making a difference on this planet, for this planet.

Melanie, Los Angeles, CA
Middle School Teacher
Married, Mother of Miles, 10, and David, 5

KIDS

Kids today are the first to come of age in an era in which the earth's health has been prioritized as an important social issue. They've internalized the green lessons they've learned at school and in popular culture, and they feel a personal connection and a sense of responsibility toward the earth. They're even taking these environmental lessons home with them, teaching—even policing—their family members. They tell Mom she's contributing to global warming by driving that gas-guzzling SUV or tell Dad that he's wasting water by taking long showers. At dinnertime, they keep an eye on who might be tossing their aluminum cans into the garbage instead of into the recycling bin. I think we're finally raising a generation of kids who will stop on the street to pick up a piece of trash—even when no one is looking.

Research shows that habits developed during childhood are likely to carry on into adulthood. This gives me hope for the future of the planet, but it's also why I believe it is so important that I, as a parent, do my part in teaching my son, Emmett, the importance of behaving responsibly and not wastefully. That can mean sending him off to school with a waste-free lunch or doing something bigger, like making an effort to always remind him of both the positive and the negative consequences of his actions. I try to be consistent with my message and say it in a way that makes sense, my hope being that he'll continue to incorporate these values as he grows up and starts doing more of his own decision making.

I know it might sound trite, but the bottom line is that today's kids will inherit this planet one day. They're the ones who eventually will be forced to face the coming environmental perils. So I believe we owe it to future generations to teach and model the proper and responsible way to live when it comes to consumption, conservation, and waste.

Parents will welcome these easy solutions that not only cut costs but also instill green habits and values in kids that will serve them well after they've moved out of the house.

VIDEO GAMES

Renter's Insurance

The SHIFT: Rent new video games instead of buying them.

Save $$: Up to $500 per year compared with buying two new video games per month.

Save the Planet: Video rentals are a great way to promote reuse, which not only saves production resources but ultimately reduces waste as well.

Good for You: Try games before purchasing them and avoid buyer's regret.

Get Used to It

The SHIFT: Instead of getting the newest generation of video game console, buy a used one from someone who is upgrading to the latest version.

Save $$: Up to $400 depending on the model.

Save the Planet: Keep functional electronics from being thrown into a landfill or from being recycled prematurely. You'll also save the plastics, metals, and fossil fuel energy used to produce the new console you decided to forgo.

Shift-it Tip: People who get rid of old consoles might also want to free themselves of games for that console. See if you can get the games thrown in for free or at least at a discount.

> ### GAME THEORY
>
> Nearly 60 million U.S. homes have at least one video game console, and the average console uses as much energy per year as two refrigerators. In all, Americans consume 16 billion kilowatt-hours of energy per year playing video games—the same amount of energy used annually by the entire city of San Diego.

Power Down

The SHIFT: When it's not in use, teach your kids to make a habit of powering down the video game console. This may mean remembering to turn the console off, or setting up the power-saving feature, which automatically powers down the device after a period of time. Leaving the console on and idle can use nearly as much energy as playing a game.

Save $$: Up to $160 per year compared with leaving the console in idle mode when not in use.

Save the Planet: Conserve up to 1,500 kilowatt-hours of electricity per year and one ton of carbon dioxide.

Shift-it Tip: If the power supply to the console is hard to reach, or you don't want your kids dealing with electric wiring, plug the console into a power strip with a timer. Set the timer so the console turns on and off at certain hours every day. This not only is a great way to save energy but also can be a strategy to limit your kids' video game time as well.

Regame

The SHIFT: Buy used video games instead of new ones.

Save $$: Up to $350 per year compared with buying two new games per month.

Save the Planet: Conserve the energy and material resources needed to make new games.

Good for You: Buying used means your kids can get more games for the same amount of money and there's less financial risk involved when trying out a game they've never played before.

SWIFT SHIFT: VINTAGE VIDEO

I don't know why anyone would buy a brand-new video game. I can get my boys the newest games—used—just a couple of weeks after they come out. When stores need to offload games they've invested in heavily for rentals, they're willing to sell them for much, much less. Sometimes I call the store and ask them to put a title away for me when it transitions from being for rent to being for purchase. Compared with buying them new, this is saving us about $350 per year. Then after the kids have had their fill of a couple of games, we invite their friends over and do a game swap. We do the same thing with our own friends for DVDs. It's a great way to get good variety without having to spend lots of money on movie and game rentals.

Melanie, Los Angeles, CA
Middle School Teacher
Married, Mother of Miles, 10, and David, 5

Game Swap

The SHIFT: If most of your kids' friends have the same video game system, you might arrange to have a video game trading party. Have the kids bring games they no longer play and trade them for games other kids are looking to unload. (This also works well with toys and board games.)

Save $$: Up to $250 per year compared with buying two used games per month.

Save the Planet: Save the manufacturing energy and inputs associated with new games. If the alternative to the trading party was selling used games online, you'll also save the materials and transportation energy used to ship the games to the new owners.

CLOTHES and TOYS

Handy-Downs

The SHIFT: Buy secondhand clothing instead of new clothing from a department store.

Save $$: Up to $250 per year or more.

Save the Planet: Conserve raw materials used for clothing manufacturing (fibers, energy, water, chemicals) and reduce waste.

Good for You: Thrift-store shopping is a great hands-on example for kids of how recycling and reusing can save materials and money.

SWIFT SHIFT:
DON'T FOLLOW TRENDS . . . START THEM!

I buy about 20 percent of my boys' clothing at secondhand stores. I estimate that this saves our family about $200 per year. When people ask me why they should buy things secondhand, I usually reply, "Why wouldn't you? If you're getting an item of good quality, what's the difference?" In fact, buying things secondhand affords you the ability to purchase higher-quality items that end up lasting longer over time. In fashion, even trends are recycled. Designers bring in ideas from the past, via inspiration from old books, catalogs, and patterns. I tell my boys to be themselves instead of following trends. Miles and David don't even notice they dress secondhand—I haven't raised them to be label snobs. Since they see both their father and me making things, they don't care about what something costs—they like creative clothes and they want to look good. We don't follow fashion in our family—we make our fashion.

Melanie, Los Angeles, CA
Middle School Teacher
Married, Mother of Miles, 10, and David, 5

SWIFT SHIFT: GET OUT!

Most kids watch lots of TV during the summer. But not ours. We shut off our cable service. Although our kids aren't looking forward to the day the television gets shut off, it's good for them. We want them to ride bikes and go to the neighborhood swimming pool for the summer, not zone out in front of the TV. By shutting down our pay-TV service for three months each year, we save $180. And even though we freeze our service, we keep our digital video recorder—and all the programming we've recorded on it. By the time the service stops, we've recorded 30 or 40 hours of cartoons from the TV, enough to keep the kids entertained in case of emergency—or rain.

Michael, Huntsville, AL
Biomedical Technician
Married, Father of Zoë, 12; Jackson, 5; and Cole, 4

Pass It On

The SHIFT: Use a website like eBay or craigslist, or search "hand me downs" for online classified services geared toward moms, to sell the toys, clothes, and other gear that your kids have outgrown.

Save $$: Recoup up to $250 per year or more depending on what you sell.

Save the Planet: Selling items secondhand gives other parents the opportunity to reuse kids' stuff instead of buying it new. This conserves material resources and energy, reduces pollution, and diminishes overall waste.

Shift-it Tip: Selling online provides you with a much larger community of buyers—and, thus, a potentially higher selling price—than having a yard sale or posting classifieds in your local paper.

SWIFT SHIFT: TOY SWAP

Despite our best efforts to be careful about our spending, there's a ton of waste that comes with having kids. We have spent so much money on toys, only to have them get broken, tossed aside, or left at random places and gone forever. After taking bags and bags of toys to Goodwill, I remember thinking, this is such a waste!

So one of the best things we did as a result of Shift Your Habit was to throw a toy-swap party. We invited all our friends' entire families to come to our house for a toy trade. We had a great time, and all the kids went home with "new" toys—absolutely free. We estimated that more than $900 worth of toys were swapped between the five families that attended. With the exception of the surplus of grimy stuffed animals, which will definitely be banned from our next toy swap, it was great to know where everything was coming from and not to have to worry about all the issues that can come from buying stuff at a thrift store. Plus, the next morning was one of the most peaceful we've ever had. Mike and I got to drink our morning coffee and relax while the boys played with their new toys—and we didn't even need to go shopping.

Melissa, Huntsville, AL
Child Life Specialist
Married, Mother of Zoë, 12; Jackson, 5: and Cole, 4

Netflix Your Toys

The SHIFT: Borrow toys online from sites instead of buying them.
Save $$: Up to $200, which is how much the average family spends per year on toys.

Save the Planet: Scaling back on the volume of toys you buy, and borrowing them instead, saves manufacturing energy, decreases plastics production—which uses petroleum and results in pollution—reduces packaging, and cuts down on nonrecyclable waste.

Good for You: Save time and your sanity by avoiding crowded toy stores. Give your kids variety without spending extra money. Avoid closets full of old toys that your kids have outgrown or grown tired of.

The Borrowers

The SHIFT: Borrow books from the library instead of buying them from a bookstore.

Save $$: Up to $200 per year for a family of four.

Save the Planet: Conserve the resources—mainly trees, water, chemicals, and energy—used to produce and transport new books, reduce air and water pollution from paper mills, and diminish the waste that comes from used books being thrown in the trash instead of being passed on to friends and family. It's hard to believe, but Americans throw away two million books per year.

Good for You: Libraries provide risk-free opportunities for trying out new authors, genres, or books that you and your kids might otherwise never read. Plus, they're a great place to spend a relaxing family afternoon—especially because of the inside voices required.

Shift-it Tip: Check out the storytelling programs your local library branch offers. Your kids can discover new authors or just listen to the children's librarian read storybooks while you recharge your batteries with some historical fiction or a magazine.

All a Board

The SHIFT: Encourage your kids to play board games instead of video games.

Save $$: Up to $20 per game.

Save the Planet: Unlike video games, most board games are made from renewable resources, use zero energy to operate, create little if any waste, and can be reused for years—even decades.

Good for You: Board games provide great opportunities to stimulate your child's young mind and foster quality interactions with friends and family while creating minimal environmental impact.

CRAFTS AND ACTIVITIES

Just Doh It

The SHIFT: Make your own Play-Doh instead of buying the name-brand stuff.

Save $$: Up to $15 on multicolored packs of store-bought Play-Doh.

Save the Planet: Avoid buying—and eventually disposing of—plastic Play-Doh containers.

Shift-it Tip: Homemade Play-Doh is inexpensive and simple to make. Try the following recipe:

> 1 cup flour
> 1 cup warm water
> 2 teaspoons cream of tartar
> 1 teaspoon oil
> ¼ cup salt
> a few drops of food coloring

Combine the flour and salt in a mixing bowl. In a glass measuring cup, mix the remaining ingredients. Add to the flour and salt mixture and stir until slightly cool. Knead well and add small amounts of additional flour until no longer sticky. Separate into small batches and use a few drops of food coloring to create colorful variations. Add a drop of peppermint, vanilla, lemon, or other food extract to give the play-dough a nice fragrance. Store in an airtight container. Empty yogurt or cottage cheese cartons are good options.

For the Birds

The SHIFT: Instead of buying bags of birdseed, make your own tasty treat for feathered friends in your community.

Even $$: Prices can be comparable.

Save the Planet: Making your own birdseed can reduce packaging waste by using products that are already in your kitchen. Also, many commercial brands of birdseed contain filler—seeds that you pay for but that birds won't eat. By making it yourself, you guarantee that you're using foods the birds will enjoy.

Shift-it Tip: Here's how to make your own homemade bird feeder: Take a pinecone. Smother it with peanut butter and roll it in oatmeal, peanut bits, or sunflower seeds. Tie a string through it and let it hang from the branch of a tree that you can view from one or more windows of your house. This feeder can attract a variety of local birds including woodpeckers, jays, nuthatches, chickadees, titmice, and even cardinals and finches.

THROW A GROCERY SCAVENGER HUNT

The best way to help your kids make the right choices when they're older is to take them to the grocery store with you when they're young. Plan a scavenger hunt—challenge them to find the most eco-friendly products available. Here are some ideas:

- Make a list of the types of materials that can be recycled in your area and teach your kids how to tell whether a particular plastic item is recyclable. Have them look for the imprinted plastics code: a number between 1 and 7 surrounded by the recycling triangle. Then have them show you some containers that can and can't be recycled.
- Ask them to point out products without packaging.
- Have them find foods packaged in reusable containers, and then suggest a new use for the empty container.
- Have them show you organic and conventional versions of the same fruit or vegetable, and figure out the price difference between the two.

MAGICAL MYSTERY TOUR

Work together to reduce your energy foot-
print at home.

Have your kids each draw a rough map
of rooms of the house. Then have them go
through each room and find the items and
appliances that are using electricity. They
can write these down or draw them on their maps. Once they've
finished, have them take you on an "energy tour" and make suggestions on how to decrease usage.

Together you can determine which incandescent bulbs need
to be replaced with compact fluorescent lights, which entertainment systems need to be plugged into power strips, and which
electronics are unused and can be unplugged altogether. Use the
tips in this book to come up with at least one way each room can
be made more energy efficient.

SCHOOL

Take Out the Trash

The SHIFT: Pack a waste-free lunch. Assemble your kids' lunches without using any disposable items or individually packaged foods.

Save $$: Up to $400 per year or more for a two-child family.

Save the Planet: Reduce waste by 90 pounds per year.

Good for You: Simply by eliminating individually packaged foods, you'll be eliminating tons of preservatives, sugars, and sodium from your lunch, without even realizing it.

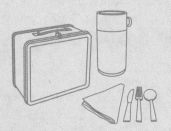

REMAKE YOUR LUNCH

Replace waste with items you can use over and over again. Here's how to dispose of those disposables.

INSTEAD OF . . .	USE . . .
A disposable brown paper bag	A reusable lunch box, canvas bag, or backpack
A drink box or plastic water bottle	A reusable thermos filled with your favorite juice or water
Paper napkins and plastic forks and spoons	A cloth napkin with actual silverware
Individual single-serving bags	Snacks in a large bag and then pack them in reusable containers
Wrapping your sandwich in a plastic Baggie	A sealed reusable sandwich container or a plastic sandwich wrap/placemat

The Popular Click

The SHIFT: Use refillable mechanical pencils instead of nonrecycled wooden pencils that need sharpening.

Even $$: Mechanical pencils are slightly more expensive than wooden pencils, but refill lead is about the same price.

Save the Planet: Some of the largest wooden pencil manufacturers have been associated with destructive logging, water and air pollution, and harming species' habitats.

Good for You: No need to sharpen dull or broken lead. No pencil shaving dust lingering in the air.

SWIFT SHIFT: LUNCH-ABLE

My younger daughter couldn't wait for school to test out her homemade make-your-own-cold-pizza kit. She started putting pizza sauce on a cracker the moment we got home from the grocery store! The girls enjoyed choosing their own foods so much they started packing their own lunches without me even needing to ask them. I am thrilled they're not eating at the school cafeteria as much as they used to. Before we became a part of Shift Your Habit, I'd often ask them what they had for lunch, and they'd answer, "French fries," which, in my opinion, is not lunch.

Since the girls are making better choices now, my husband and I figured we should, too. So we joined an online weight-loss club. Since we're not eating on the fly, we're thinking about what we're putting in our bodies—and, so far, fingers crossed, it's working.

Samantha, Orange County, CA
Insurance Company Project Manager
Married, Mother of Allison, 15, and Kellie, 9

SWIFT SHIFT: TRASH-FREE CLASS

My son, Emmett, is in third grade, and he and his classmates are always game for an eco-challenge. So I gave students and teachers alike the opportunity to demonstrate just how low they could go when it came to reducing classroom waste. Their starting point was 12.5 pounds of trash per day—or about 2,250 pounds total for the school year. Over the course of a week, the teachers joined me in teaching the kids about waste reduction, reusing, and recycling. Over the next week, they transitioned to completely eliminating the use of paper (except for homework packets), using only washable glasses instead of disposable cups, and switching to green cleaning products with washable rags instead of paper towels. They were also sent home with instructions on how to pack a trash-free lunch. By the end of the three-week challenge, classroom waste production fell from 12.5 pounds per day to just 2 pounds per day—a reduction of 84%. But it wasn't just the results that the kids were impressed with. According to Genevieve, one of their teachers, the exercise really did change the students' point of view:

Seeing how much less packaging students bring in their lunches and snacks has been amazing—they've made a strong commitment to reusable containers and water bottles. Some continue to use plastic water bottles but at least reuse the bottle several times before tossing it in the blue bin. I love walking by the snack area and hearing a kid yelp to a classmate, "Wait! That can be recycled!"

There has also been a strong internal shift in the way students think about the environment. They are making meaningful connections between our study of ecosystems in science and the real world that they live in. They are looking for recycling containers everywhere they go. Yesterday, on

*our field trip to an art museum, several children chose to
carry their empty water bottles back to school because the
museum did not have recycling bins readily available.
Several students have commented that they had family
meetings about what they can do to be more conscious of
the amount of trash they create.*

*Based on the statistics that Elizabeth provided, students
came away with the overarching message of the project:
"If our class can create so much trash in a week, then what
does that mean about the amount of trash created by the
world?" And by the same token, each of them understands
that if one child or one family works toward shifting their
habits, then maybe one day every child and every family will
be making daily choices that protect our planet.*

Genevieve, Los Angeles, CA
Teacher, Married

Change Is Instrumental

The SHIFT: Rent, borrow, or buy used musical instruments instead
of buying new ones.

Save $$: Up to $400 or more.

Save the Planet: Help conserve the energy and resources used to
make a new instrument and make good use of a used one that
would likely otherwise sit gathering dust in a closet or attic—
and eventually get thrown away.

Good for You: Your kids will understand that a major purchase takes
time and deliberation if you allow them to borrow and try a va-
riety of instruments before choosing the one they like best.
You'll show them that investing in something means you owe
it a long-term commitment. Also, you won't be out half a rent
check just because Jimmy discovers the reed makes his teeth
hurt.

Shift-it Tip: If you bought an instrument that your child subsequently abandoned, sell it used to the parent of an elementary school student, a music store, or online.

SWIFT SHIFT: SHIFTING OUR HABITS!

After working with Emmett's fellow classmates on shifting their habits, two of them wrote an article about it in a newsletter that went out to the parents.

Lately we have been working on shifting our habits with Elizabeth (Emmett's mom). She said that the average amount of trash produced by one classroom a year is 2,250 pounds! That is equal to . . . the weight of a full-grown cow . . . the total weight of 35 average 9-year-olds . . . or the total weight of one million one-dollar bills!

Elizabeth is a woman who wants to make a difference, and as long as it will take, we won't let her down. She is committed to this and we owe her. We owe the world. The Earth provides us with food, water, and shelter, our three basic needs. If we don't go trash-free, it's possible that all of those things might be gone in a few million years (that is just an estimate).

Shifting our habits is a great thing because when we succeed, we will take what we have learned and share that with family, friends, neighbors, and more! Just by changing the classroom habits, we are actually changing a lot of people too! If we got more and more people to do it throughout the world, it would make a huge difference.

Thank you for reading this article. We hope you help make a difference too.

Sophia, 10, and Emily, 10, Los Angeles, CA
Fourth-Grade Students

Play It Again

The SHIFT: Buy used sports equipment instead of ordering every-thing brand-new.

Save $$: Up to $300 per year depending on the type and quantity of sporting goods purchased.

Save the Planet: Sporting goods can be expensive because their pro-duction is both energy and resource intensive. So when you buy used goods, you're conserving the inputs that would oth-erwise go into making new sports equipment.

Good for You: Buying less-expensive used goods—and having the option of selling them back—provides you with more financial leeway when your kids are taking up a new sport every week.

SWIFT SHIFT: EATING BY EXAMPLE

As part of our shifts, my boys and I pledged to pack waste-free lunches for school each day. I estimate it's probably saving us close to $500 per year. My youngest son, David, had a hard time giving up the little plastic Baggies that used to hold his snacks, until he fell even more in love with the tiny washable containers that replaced them. For me personally, I found it hilarious when I took my lunch to work one day and my seventh-grade students spied my colorful reusable sandwich wrapper mat and exclaimed, "What the hell is that?" They looked as if I had brought an alien to school. I explained to them what I was doing and about the project. After that day, they began monitoring my lunch to make sure that I wasn't cheating by using zipper-lock bags or by drinking from a disposable water bottle.

Melanie, Los Angeles, CA
Middle School Teacher
Married, Mother of Miles, 10, and David, 5

SWIFT SHIFT: VICIOUS CYCLER

Our seven-year-old son, Tydeman, wants to be just like his dad, who rides his bike everywhere. So, of course, Tydeman rides his bike everywhere, too—even to school. It's very inspiring, but sometimes I fear we may have created a monster! Tydeman recently declared that he simply doesn't like cars. He loves to ride to school and gets very cross about the big cars taking up space, and to anyone who will listen he'll say, "It's really not right, people driving such big cars when they live so close to where they're going." He actually thinks people shouldn't be allowed to have cars at all and enjoys talking about how he'll never have a car. Let's see if he feels the same way when he's sixteen. Hopefully, by then electric vehicles will be easily accessible to everyone.

Naomi, Woodland Hills, CA
Married
Stay-at-Home Mother of Tydeman, 7; Jonesy, 5; and Poppy, 3

I Like Bike

The SHIFT: Bike to school with your kids.

Save $$: Up to $220 by biking to school three times a week, on average, instead of driving.

Save the Planet: Conserve more than 55 gallons of gas per school year.

Good for You: Save driving time and avoid getting stuck in school drop-off traffic. And it's a great way to get a little extra exercise.

Walk This Way

The SHIFT: If you live in a safe neighborhood within a mile of your kids' school, have them walk to school—or walk with them—at least a few days a week.

Save $$: Up to $40 per school year.

Save the Planet: Save about 10 gallons of gas per school year.

Good for You: Walking to and from school will fulfill most of the 30 minutes of daily exercise recommended by doctors. Plus, studies show that the brain works more efficiently after exercise—something about getting that blood pumping?—so waking up your kids with a brisk walk may even improve their school performance.

SWIFT SHIFT: PAPER TRAIL

The school where I work doesn't do anything to recycle or conserve natural resources. Becoming a part of Shift Your Habit made me aware of what I could do to get things started. Before the project, I used a ton of copy paper for my class. Now I'm doing what I can to cut back, like using both sides of the paper and turning old handouts into scrap paper. I've even taught my students to do the same. Although this does not save me money personally, I know it is saving the school money. And in this state budget climate, every dollar counts.

Melanie, Los Angeles, CA
Middle School Teacher
Married, Mother of Miles, 10, and David, 5

Get on the Bus!

The SHIFT: Instead of driving them yourself, have your kids take the bus to school. If you're not making use of your school's bus program, investigate it and sign up. Or, if you live along a municipal bus route, ride the bus to school with your kids.

Save $$: Up to $400 on gas costs if you live 3 miles from school and make two round trips from home every day of the school year.

Save the Planet: Conserve nearly 100 gallons of gas or more.

Good for You: Save time driving to school and back—up to 180 hours or more per year. Teach your kids the importance of developing habits that are good for saving money and for the environment. And develop friendships with other folks who ride the bus! Make your kids really feel a part of their community.

SWIFT SHIFT: MILES FOR MILES

My older son, Miles, goes to a school that's about 45 minutes away from where we live. I used to drive him in, fighting the crowded LA freeways every morning and afternoon, but fortunately now there's a bus program. I simply drop him off on my way to work at the stop near our house. Miles loves riding the bus. He feels a sense of confidence and independence being out in the world by himself. And of course I have peace of mind knowing he's safe and protected. The bus also teaches him responsibility—there are consequences if he misses it! Now that I can head home before rush hour, I get home sooner because I miss the traffic. I'm also saving about $1,500 per year at the pump.

Melanie, Los Angeles, CA
Middle School Teacher
Married, Mother of Miles, 10, and David, 5

BABIES

Puree Genius

The SHIFT: Make your own baby food instead of buying it in jars at the supermarket.

Save $$: Up to $1,500 per year.

Save the Planet: Conserve resources by forgoing the purchase of individually packaged single-serving jars of food for your child.

Good for You: Choose the ingredients you know your child loves. Whip up a batch of baby food with local, organic fruits and vegetables, or pick them fresh and ripe from your edible garden.

Shift-it Tip: To freeze homemade baby food, pour puree into ice cube trays and freeze. Once they're frozen, place cubes in a sealed and labeled container in the freezer. When it's mealtime, just take out one or two cubes to thaw and serve to your little one.

Cut from the Same Cloth

The SHIFT: Use cloth diapers instead of disposable ones.

Save $$: Up to $1,700 per year for three years.

Save the Planet: Reduce the resources used to make the disposable diapers, as well as the waste you send to the landfill each year.

Good for You: Most disposable diapers are whitened with chlorine bleach, which is harmful to the environment and can irritate a baby's skin. Washing your own diapers keeps you in control of the chemicals your baby's behind is exposed to.

Shift-it Tip: Cloth diapers can be reused for additional children or passed on to other parents. Certain all-in-one brands of cloth diapers have high resale value. If the idea of cloth diapers appeals to you but you can't imagine keeping them clean, it may be worth your time to check the prices of diaper services in your area.

Vintage **Baby**

Baby strollers are like cars—they lose most of their resale value the minute you drive them off the lot. So do other must-haves, from cribs to changing tables, bassinets to bouncers.

We shopped online for new and used versions of six key items—identical models and brands—and found an average of 60 percent savings.

Check out the deals we found here:

Item	New price	Used price	Savings
Sleigh crib	$1,000	$300	$700
Changing table	$115	$50	$65
Bassinet	$210	$105	$105
Stroller	$190	$125	$65
Bouncer	$85	$55	$30
Folding bouncer/rocker	$85	$60	$25
Total spent	**$1,655**	**$655**	**$990**

The Answer Is Clear

The SHIFT: Buy glass baby bottles instead of plastic ones.

Save $$: Up to $60 compared to buying a set of six bisphenol A (BPA) bottles.

Save the Planet: Glass bottles are 100% reusable and recyclable, whereas plastic bottles are made from petroleum and can't be recycled into new ones.

Good for You: Glass bottles don't leach chemicals like plastic bottles do. BPA, found in some types of plastic bottles, is linked to neurological and reproductive disorders in laboratory animals, which researchers say may be associated with increased risk of prostate cancer, breast cancer, ovarian cysts, endometriosis, and early-onset puberty in humans.

Shift-it Tip: Prevent breakage by getting a foam sleeve to cover your glass baby bottle.

SWIFT SHIFT: THE GREEN WOMB

Right around the time we started shifting, we found out we were pregnant. Nauseated-morning-noon-and-night-sickness pregnant! It has been an interesting ride for Jill— change the lightbulb, meet the toilet, take the recycling out, meet the toilet. But we're excited about everything we're learning and look forward to teaching our child about green ideas at an early age.

Jeremy, Orlando, FL
Realtor
Married, Pet Lover, and Parent-to-Be

Neutralizer

The SHIFT: Choose a gender-neutral color for baby gear and accessories for ease of reuse with baby number two, or for resale.

Save $$: Up to $500 or more.

Save the Planet: Keep half as many bumpers and buggies going to the landfill.

Good for You: Save the time and energy spent choosing new nursery decor.

Wipe In

The SHIFT: Use a reusable, washable cloth instead of baby wipes.

Save $$: Up to $100 per year if cloths are washed in the same loads with cloth diapers.

Save the Planet: Keep an estimated 2,500 baby wipes—along with their chemical cleansers, plastic containers, and packaging—out of the landfill.

Good for You: Baby wipes are treated with alcohol-based cleaners, which can dry out and irritate your baby's sensitive skin.

Shift-it Tip: If you prefer store-bought baby wipes, choose the refill packages instead of the clamshell hard plastic packages. You'll reduce waste and save about $60 per year.

Sure I Wood

The SHIFT: Avoid plastic baby toys—especially teething rings or other toys made from soft, gummy polyvinyl chloride (PVC) or vinyl. Buy unfinished, unpainted, or lead-free painted wooden toys instead.

It's Worth it: Although wood toys can be expensive, they last longer and retain their resale value.

Save the Planet: Plastic toys have short shelf lives because they're low quality and inexpensive. Buying more soundly made wooden toys keeps those unwanted or broken plastic toys out of the waste stream.

Good for You: PVC contains phthalates, which are associated with a number of reproductive and developmental disorders.

Shift-it Tip: If you buy plastic toys, look for "PVC-free" and "phthalate-free" labels to avoid the risks associated with plastic chemicals.

KIDS: The Bottom Line

Make these shifts and save up to **$8,000** or more!

For additional ways to raise your kids green and to discuss lunch boxes and toy-swap parties, check out http://shiftyourhabit.com.

MEET THE SHIFTERS:

Jill and Jeremy

Jeremy and Jill, devoted "parents" of three cats and a dog who rule their lives, are awaiting the birth of their first (human) baby. They want to start their baby's life off right, making choices and purchases consciously and responsibly.

A big part of our life has always been taking care of our pets, and soon it's going to be caring for our new baby. Because money will be tighter than ever, this pregnancy has been the perfect time to take some major steps toward living simply and becoming more financially responsible.

Although to some degree we've always cared about preserving the environment, there's been a disconnect between our desire to take action and actually following through. Since we'd like to introduce good habits to our child from the very beginning, the opportunity to be part of Shift Your Habit seemed like the perfect chance for us to practice self-discipline and finally go green. But starting off wasn't as easy as we thought it would be.

There were so many things to remember at the beginning: Did I turn off the lights? Use cloth towels, not paper towels; take the motorcycle to work instead of the car; eat leftovers instead of ordering takeout. Is that concentrated high-efficiency detergent? Is this brand of cat litter eco-friendly? It was a lot of self-observation. So it's true that we've had to make some sacrifices, but it's been worth it. We're already seeing huge payoffs.

This whole experience has reminded us that we have brains, they work, and we can reprogram them. The more we practice these shifts, the more we condition ourselves to make the better choice in whatever we do, which spills into other aspects of our lives. It hasn't all been easy, but we're more aware than we used to be. Still, we're always thinking twice before doing anything and tease each other if something is not "very green." We think we'll probably share a lot more giggles in the near future, but at least we're finally on the right track.

Jill and Jeremy, Orlando, FL
Medical Administrator and Realtor
Pet Lovers and Parents-to-Be

PETS

The proven emotional and health benefits pets provide make them worth their weight in gold—or at least in chew toys. Studies have repeatedly shown that having a pet can reduce an owner's blood pressure, stress, cholesterol, and triglyceride levels. Survival rates of pet owners who were hospitalized for heart problems have been found to be four times higher than those of ailing people without pets. People who suffer from loneliness and depression also experience fewer symptoms once they get a pet. This might be partly due to the fact that a pet refuses to let its owner stay in bed all day. Pets demand attention—needing to be walked, fed, played with, and nurtured—and these are all opportunities for exercise, outdoor activity, and socialization.

Given all your pet does for you, you certainly want to do the best for your pet. But too often the best is unaffordable. Especially, it seems, when it comes to healthy pet products that are also better for the planet. In fact, sometimes having a pet can seem as expensive as having a child! (I should know—I have three children, and only one of them is human.)

Read on to find ways to cut your pet's impact on your bottom line—and on the earth—while improving your pet's quality of life.

Take a Walk

The SHIFT: If you're paying someone to walk your dog a few times a week, why not do it yourself?

Save $$: Up to $1,800 per year or more if your dog is walked three times per week.

Save the Planet: Unless your dog walker lives down the street, she is probably driving to your house in order to walk your dog. So when you do it yourself, you save the fuel and the pollution associated with your dog walker's transportation.

Good for You: Walking your dog is great exercise for you as well as for your dog. And if you just can't get yourself up early enough to take the dog for a walk, consider this: People who are active fall asleep more quickly and get better-quality sleep than people who are sedentary. So test it out and see if a little morning exercise helps you get your z's. It may just be a win-win!

Planned Parenthood

The SHIFT: If it's not already taken care of, make sure you get your pet spayed or neutered.

Save $$: Up to $1,000 if the alternative is either increased health care for your pet, or a litter of kittens or puppies to care for.

Save the Planet: Reducing involuntary breeding among stray animals reduces the number of unwanted animals that are sent to pounds and put to sleep. Some 3.5 million unwanted cats are euthanized in the United States every year.

Good for You: Spaying and neutering help dogs and cats live longer, healthier lives by eliminating the possibility of uterine, ovarian, or testicular cancer, and decreasing the incidence of prostate disease.

Early Adopter

The SHIFT: Instead of buying your new friend from a pet store or breeder, adopt one from a shelter.

Save $$: Up to $500 depending on animal and breed.

Save the Planet: Adopting a shelter pet not only saves a life but also reduces demand for purebred animals, which are more likely to have medical problems owing to genetic abnormalities.

Good for You: Adopting an orphaned animal keeps it from having to be euthanized. Most shelter animals are spayed or neutered, have been treated for worms, and have at least their first set of shots. If you're not willing to go through the trials of house-training a young puppy or kitten, an older shelter animal is a good option.

Shift-it Tip: If you're set on a purebred dog or cat, buy one from a rescue association instead of getting a pedigree from a breeder. Contact the Humane Society of the United States to locate a nearby rescue group.

Tank You, I'm Crateful

The SHIFT: Buy used aquariums, terrariums, crates, and cages for your pets.

Save $$: Up to $300 depending on size and type.

Save the Planet: Aquariums have few other uses besides holding animals or gathering dust. If not used, they're eventually tossed in the garbage, as their multiple parts make them difficult to recycle—especially if they're made of Plexiglas. For crates and cages, the mining of metals involves blasting earth and mountainsides, which results in disrupted ecosystems and contaminated water bodies.

Room? Don't Board

The SHIFT: Instead of boarding your pets in a kennel, ask a friend to mind your pets while you're away.

Save the Planet: Managing a pet-boarding facility requires more water and energy than does keeping your pet home with a sitter.

Good for You: Keeping your pets in their familiar environment is much less stressful on them than boarding them in a strange place with strange caretakers.

A Real Meal

Shift-it Tip: As tempting as it might be, don't buy the cheapest pet food available. Most of the generic and discounted varieties contain high-calorie filler, which may lead to hyperactivity and won't provide your pet with the nutrients essential to his or her healthy growth and longevity.

Save $$: Up to $250 on extra training costs or vet expenses over the course of your pet's lifetime.

Save the Planet: Fewer trips to visit specialists means fewer resources used for treatment and lower gas consumption driving there.

Incredible Bulk

The SHIFT: Buy flea and tick medicine and any other pet medications online and in bulk instead of buying them one month at a time from your vet.

Save $$: Up to $125 per year.

Save the Planet: Buying a 12-month supply reduces packaging waste and also conserves the fuel you'd normally use to pick up your pet's meds every month or two.

Good for You: Save time driving and sitting in waiting rooms at the vet's office.

SWIFT SHIFT: PET READY

Because we have four pets—three cats and a dog—we are all too familiar with the waiting room at the vet's office. But individual visits with each pet can really add up. We were so excited to find a veterinarian willing to make house calls and check in on all four pets at once, and for just a little more than the price of one office visit. And that doesn't count the money we're saving from not driving back and forth from the office. Not to mention it's so much easier and more convenient—schlepping the cats is impossible! We can barely keep them in the house as is. We also started buying our pets' medications in bulk online instead of at the pet store or the vet's office. Jeremy is trying to make the cats some homemade scratch pads in order to spare the expensive furniture they keep tearing to shreds—but the jury's still out on whether the cats will enjoy them as much as they enjoy the couch.

Jill and Jeremy, Orlando, FL
Medical Administrator and Realtor
Pet Lovers and Parents-to-Be

Fun from Scratch

The SHIFT: Buy a scratching pad made from recycled materials that resemble a tree trunk.

Save $$: Up to $40 over an upright scratching post covered with carpeting.

Save the Planet: Products made with recycled content reduce the need for raw materials to produce new items and keep used materials out of the landfill.

Shift-it Tip: Any scratching post sure beats having your furniture ruined by an overzealous tabby.

Sleep Well

The SHIFT: Buy a pet bed made with polyester spun from recycled plastic bottles instead of a standard pet bed with a cotton or suede cover and virgin polyester fill.

Save $$: Up to $35.

Save the Planet: Reduce manufacturing energy by up to 85% and save hundreds of plastic bottles from going to landfills.

Shift-it Tip: If you can't find recycled items in your local pet supply shop, there are lots of eco-friendly pet supply stores online. You can also try making your own pet bed out of old blankets, pillows, or couch cushions.

SWIFT SHIFT: NOT-SO-FANCY CLANCY

Because Clancy used to be my dad's dog—I inherited him when my dad passed away—I want him to have the best of everything. But in talking with Elizabeth, I realized that I was confused about what kinds of experiences would really make a difference in Clancy's life. I was spending about $200 per year on fancy dog toys, which more often than not got lost, destroyed, or abandoned. Elizabeth pointed out that even though they're small, dog toys involve resource consumption and eventually end up as waste. So Clancy has shifted his habits away from plastic pet-store toys in order to be a more eco-friendly pooch. It turns out that he's much more interested in playing with empty cardboard boxes or old tennis balls anyway.

Molly, Santa Monica, CA
Manager of a Breast Cancer Foundation
Married, Clancy's Mom

Toy Story

The SHIFT: You know how babies love to play with keys more than any other expensive toy made just for them? Pets are the same way. Instead of buying toys, you can delight dogs and cats with stuff you already own.

Save $$: Up to $200 per year on pet toys.

Save the Planet: Creating pet toys from items you'd otherwise throw away reduces manufacturing energy as well as waste, since you'll be buying fewer toys overall and tossing fewer destroyed toys into the garbage.

Shift-it Tip: Here are a few ideas to entertain your pooch or feline: knotted-up old towels, cut-up sheets, holey T-shirts, or other rags for tug-of-war; old—or orphaned—socks stuffed with catnip; cardboard boxes or paper towel rolls; old tennis or racquet balls; string; ponytail holders.

Bone-a-Fide

The SHIFT: Give your dog real marrow bones instead of rawhide or bones manufactured from nylon—a synthetic material made from petroleum products. Many animal experts say rawhide bones are not the best choice for your dog's health—not to mention the fact that they're expensive and get gobbled up in a day. You can get marrow bones from your local butcher as scraps or at most pet stores. Keep them in the freezer when your pup isn't gnawing away. Compared with other bones that might last a week, real marrow bones can last for months.

Save $$: Up to $50 per year if your pooch gets a new rawhide bone every three to four days.

Save the Planet: Buying scraps from the butcher is the perfect example of recycling and repurposing an item that would otherwise be discarded as waste. And because you're buying direct, you avoid the environmental effects of processing, packaging, and transporting the manufactured bones sold at the pet store.

Shift-it Tip: Although few health problems result from dogs chewing on real bones, there is always the remote possibility that bone pieces will break off. Thus, it's recommended that owners supervise their dogs when they're chewing on bones and remove any small pieces that may splinter off.

Go Fishing for Water

The SHIFT: When cleaning your aquarium, use the old water to feed your plants instead of pouring it down the drain. Aquarium water contains high levels of nitrogen and other nutrients that plants need to grow.

Save $$: Up to $15 per year on fertilizer costs.

Save the Planet: Save the energy, pollution, and mining waste that comes from manufacturing synthetic fertilizers. Conserve transportation fuels, and reduce the amount of packaging that must be disposed of.

Shift-it Tip: Do not use fish tank water for houseplants if you have a saltwater tank or add any types of chemicals to the aquarium water to balance pH or to kill algae.

Veg In

The SHIFT: Buy vegetarian pet food instead of meat-based pet food.

It's Worth It: Vegetarian pet food may be 15–20 cents more per pound than nonvegetarian pet food.

Save the Planet: Vegetarian diets require less energy, water, and land resources to produce. They also result in less waste.

Good for Them: Pets given vegetarian food may be healthier and less disease prone than pets fed meat-based products, so even though you may have to lay out more cash, it could pay off in the long run.

It's in the Bag!

The SHIFT: Buy compostable dog-waste bags instead of using plastic bags to dispose of dog waste.

It's Worth It: The average cost is 10 cents per bag, which could cost about $35 per year if you use one per day.

Save the Planet: Allow dog waste to break down the way nature intended, instead of immortalizing it forever in a plastic bag buried in a landfill.

Shift-it Tip: The bags are designed so that both the waste and the bag can be thrown in your backyard compost or in your curbside green-waste bin. Check with your local waste hauler to confirm that biodegradable bags and pet waste can be disposed of with other compostable items.

Coconuts for Substrate

The SHIFT: Instead of padding your pet's cage with redwood bark or other wood chips, try a coconut husk substrate. It's good for hamsters, guinea pigs, mice, rats, rabbits and ferrets, turtles, snakes, lizards, frogs, and spiders.

Even $$: Prices can be comparable.

Save the Planet: Coconut husk cage shavings are made from materials that would have otherwise been discarded, so they save raw resources and reduce waste.

Shift-it Tip: Coconut husk substrate is billed as a product that can be used in wet or dry cages. It controls odor, doesn't rot or mildew, and contains no artificial colors or fragrances. It's long lasting and is said to promote breeding (if that's your plan).

Hemp Wanted

The SHIFT: Buy a pet collar made from hemp instead of a nylon or leather collar.

It's Worth It: Hemp collars may cost $3–$7 more, but they are more durable and will last longer than synthetic or nylon ones.

Save the Planet: Hemp is a strong material made from renewable plant fibers, whereas nylon is made from petroleum, a nonrenewable material.

SWIFT SHIFT: LAB COAT

I used to take my black Lab, Clancy, to the groomer every other month. This was a pricey indulgence, but I justified the cost and the absurd amount of water consumed by telling myself that Clancy enjoyed the experience and that it was necessary to keep his gorgeous coat looking top-notch. Then Elizabeth asked if I'd ever used the FURminator, which is a comblike instrument that you rake through your pet's coat to free all the loose hair that's been shed (it doesn't cut anything, just loosens it). Well let me just say that my first experience with this magical instrument was mind blowing. I couldn't believe the tufts that came off Clancy! Given that this shift is saving me about $600 per year, I don't see any reason to go back to the groomer. I love grooming Clancy myself, and I can't believe I waited this long to do it.

Molly, Santa Monica, CA
Manager of a Breast Cancer Foundation
Married, Clancy's Mom

Litter Naturally

The SHIFT: Buy plant-based cat litter instead of clay-based or silica-based cat litter.

It's Worth It: Eco-friendly cat litter may cost 25 cents more per pound, but it lasts longer than the clay-based products.

Save the Planet: Many plant-based cat litters are 100% recycled from scrap plant, tea, and wood materials in various manufacturing facilities.

Good for You: Plant-based cat litter is naturally odor absorbing and doesn't require the use of synthetic chemicals and fragrances.

PETS: The Bottom Line

Make these shifts and save up to **$4,300** or more!

For further ideas that make taking care of your pet a walk in the park, and to talk about homemade pet toys, check out http://shiftyourhabit.com.

MEET THE SHIFTER:
Brooke

Brooke is founder and owner of an agency that manages artists working in hair, makeup, and wardrobe styling. Over the past couple of years she made the shift to running her offices in Los Angeles and New York City with more attention to environmental responsibility.

Having grown up in Vancouver, British Columbia, I care deeply about preserving the planet that shaped who I am as a person. And luckily, the people within the creative community —hair and makeup artists, actors, and fashion designers—are usually receptive to opening their minds to change.

I give The Green Book *a tremendous amount of credit for my running the business the way I do. What instantly vibrated with me was the simplicity of how changing just one aspect of what I did every day could affect the world in a much bigger way. Having someone figure out the cumulative effect of the little things was really helpful. I handed out* The Green Book *as a guide to everybody in the office.*

What shocked me most about participating in Shift Your Habit was the amount of money my office is saving by operating the way we do—over $17,000 per year! I would probably run a green office even if it cost me money, but the fact that I'm saving money makes me feel as though the universe is rewarding me for my good deeds.

Brooke, New York City
Founder and Owner of a Creative Services Management Agency

WORK

The average American employee spends more waking hours per weekday on the job than at home. So it's no wonder that work can feel like a second life, totally separate from the one we live when we're with our friends and family. As such, it can be really easy to check our environmental—and cost—consciousness at the revolving door.

In fact, a study conducted by Harris Interactive showed that Americans who make an effort to be eco-friendly at home don't necessarily do so at work. Those of us who would never consider using a paper cup at home—who are religious about recycling our cans and shutting off our lights—turn into wild wasties when we're at work. We take a new Dixie cup every time we venture to the water cooler. We embrace single-serving everything. We leave the lights, music, and computers on in our empty offices and conference rooms. Unfortunately, it's much easier not to worry about being wasteful when operating on somebody else's dime.

When I consult with business owners and employees in office environments about going green, they're consistently amazed by all of the opportunities that exist for their office community to make a difference for the planet, while cutting costs significantly.

If your company doesn't have eco-friendly practices in place, there's nothing wrong with offering to help implement them. Consider setting up an energy audit to determine how the company can reduce energy consumption. Start a recycling program. Plan a service day to clean up a local park or plant trees. For the corporations I've worked with, I've found that a real sense of community comes out of collaborating toward a more responsible way to work—and live.

Read on for everything you need to know about how to make your office work for you and your budget, while having a gentler—maybe even positive!—impact on the planet.

The OFFICE ENVIRONMENT

Lights Out

The SHIFT: If they're not on a motion timer, turn off the lights in your office when you leave work at lunchtime or night. Encourage the last person who leaves to turn off the lights in hallways, kitchens, breakrooms, and conference rooms.

Save $$: Turning off the lights in the equivalent of 25 offices or cubicles every night saves about $5,000 per year in electricity costs.

Save the Planet: Conserve more than 60,000 kilowatt-hours of energy per year and nearly 38 tons of carbon dioxide.

Good for You: Save yourself—or your company's maintenance crew—time buying and replacing lightbulbs or ballasts.

SWIFT SHIFT: HOW ILLUMINATING

We replaced all of our standard lightbulbs with CFLs [compact fluorescent lights]. While I know everybody's always talking about fluorescent lighting being unflattering, I really don't think the quality of our lighting has changed much at all. Our ceilings are extremely high, and we need a bright atmosphere, so energy-saving bulbs work really well for us. I estimate that between our two offices, we're saving almost $1,000 per year.

Brooke, New York City
Founder and Owner of a Creative Services Management Agency

Light Bright

The SHIFT: Use natural lighting instead of overheads and desk lamps. Obviously this works only if you're lucky enough to sit

near a window—so if you don't have one yet, let this tip serve
as motivation to fight hard for that promotion!

Save $$: Up to $1,000 per year on electricity costs for a company
with five window offices—much more for an office that's
bigger.

Save the Planet: Save more than 12,000 kilowatt-hours of energy per
year and 7.5 tons of carbon dioxide emissions.

Good for You: Substantial research has found a relationship between
artificial lighting (or lack of natural light) and several undesir-
able health effects including depression, increased stress,
headaches, afternoon tiredness, sleep disturbances, and con-
centration and learning difficulties. People who work in nat-
ural lighting have been shown to be more productive, report
greater levels of satisfaction toward their work and their lives,
and stay in better moods.

Shift-it Tip: If you don't have access to natural lighting, consider get-
ting a full-spectrum lamp, which mimics sunlight. It isn't quite
the same as having a window office, but it can be effective at
reducing or eliminating some of the problems associated with
artificial lighting.

SWIFT SHIFT: FROG DAYS OF SUMMER

*In our office we try to be very mindful of our consumption.
We turn off all heating and air-conditioning at night and on
weekends. Because we're a bunch of women, we hardly use
the air-conditioning anyway. Sometimes I'll come into the
office and say, "You guys, are you frogs? It's a hundred
degrees in here, have you not noticed?" But I'm not
complaining—we're saving lots of money and energy.*

Brooke, New York City
Founder and Owner of a Creative Services Management Agency

Weekend Respite

The SHIFT: Turn off air-conditioning and heat at night and on weekends.

Save $$: Up to $3,000 per year for an average small business in a single office.

Save the Planet: Conserve up to 38,000 kilowatt-hours or more of electricity.

COMPUTERS and OFFICE EQUIPMENT

Shut It Down

The SHIFT: Shut down the computers in your office at the end of each workday instead of leaving them on throughout the night.

Save $$: Up to $1,600 per year on energy costs for an office with 25 computers.

Save the Planet: Conserve 20,000 kilowatt-hours of electricity per year, and reduce carbon dioxide emissions by 12.5 tons annually.

Good for You: It's an old myth that turning your computer off and starting it up again causes wear and tear. What actually causes your hard drive to age is overheating—and obviously a computer that's shut down is much cooler than one left running.

Go to Sleep

The SHIFT: Activate your computer's power management tool to send your machine into sleep mode after ten minutes of inactivity.

Save $$: Up to $350 per year on energy costs for a company that activates power management on 25 computers.

Save the Planet: Conserve up to 4,500 kilowatt-hours of energy and 3 tons of carbon dioxide.

Good for You: Putting your computer into sleep mode saves just as much energy as turning off the monitor, but it does this automatically so you don't have to worry about leaving it on.

REJECT RESPONSIBLY

The volume of computer products discarded in the United States has grown steadily over the last decade, increasing by an average of about 20,000 tons per year. Americans disposed of just over 82,000 tons of computers in 1999. By 2007 the amount had nearly tripled to 244,000 tons. Of course I don't expect you to hold on to your obsolete computer—the last thing we need is a bunch of cheap environmentalists plunking along on their Commodore 64s—but please donate or responsibly recycle any machine you upgrade.

Save Your Screen

The SHIFT: Say sayonara to your screensaver. Setting your power management to activate a screensaver after a period of being idle can be a huge waste of energy—especially if the screensaver runs all night. In most cases, screensavers use more energy than a computer consumes while it's being used. Instead, set your computer to go into sleep or stand-by mode.

Save $$: For an office with 25 computers, save $400 per year by activating sleep mode instead of a screensaver during the workday.

Save the Planet: Save up to 5,000 kilowatt-hours and more than 6,000 pounds of carbon dioxide.

Good for You: Screensavers were originally invented to prevent something called phosphor burn, which "etched" long-standing images into the screen. Phosphor burn is no longer much of a concern on today's monitors, so you can turn the lights out on your virtual aquarium.

The Upside of Download

The SHIFT: Buy downloadable software online instead of software on CD or DVD.

Save $$: Up to $25 per program.

Save the Planet: Save gas by eliminating the need to drive to an office supply store or have software delivered to your home. Save the resources required to produce the disks, packaging, and booklets that accompany boxes of software, as well as the waste they generate upon disposal.

Good for You: You'll save tons of time as a result of the instant download. And since you'll need to register with the software company, you'll be able to redownload if your computer crashes. One less thing to worry about: no need to keep track of and store physical software and the accompanying piles of paper materials.

Disk Dive

The SHIFT: Buy rewritable DVDs to back up your data instead of an external hard drive.

Save $$: Up to $300 for 100 gigabytes of data storage.

Save the Planet: DVDs require less energy and fewer resources to manufacture, and they consume less energy during backup.

Good for You: DVDs are easier to store and are more convenient for laptop users since using them for data backup does not require an external power supply.

SWIFT SHIFT: WHAT AN E-WASTE

I'm really concerned about the pollution being caused by e-waste, so we've chosen to donate all of our used computers and office equipment to local schools, and we give our old cell phones to women's centers or police stations for reuse. This keeps working electronics from being sent to a landfill—where toxic components will eventually leak—or from being sent to a third-world recycler, where both human health and environmental health are at risk from careless dismantling processes.

Brooke, New York City
Founder and Owner of a Creative Services Management Agency

Winning Lap

The SHIFT: Buy a laptop computer instead of a desktop computer with a monitor.

Save $$: After the initial cost difference, laptops use a fraction of the energy consumed by a desktop computer and external monitor, saving you about $45 in electricity costs per year.

Save the Planet: Conserve roughly 450 kilowatt-hours of electricity per year—enough to run a laptop 10 hours per day for 5 years. Also, laptops require fewer resources to produce and less waste to eventually recycle.

Good for You: Today's laptops have the same functionality and power as most desktops, but because they are small and portable, they're more convenient.

Three in One

The SHIFT: Buy an all-in-one printer, scanner, and fax machine instead of separate machines for your home or business office.

Save $$: Up to $400 or more in initial purchase costs, and about $40 in energy costs per year.

Save the Planet: Energy savings equal roughly 400 kilowatt-hours per year, enough to power four 100-watt lightbulbs for 100 days straight. Buying fewer machines also reduces manufacturing resources, energy, and waste.

Good for You: Conserve space!

Just the Fax, Ma'am

The SHIFT: Use an online, electronic fax service instead of buying a fax machine. You'll no longer need to pay for a dedicated phone line, or supply a paper tray, or worry about jams or transmission errors. Faxes sent to your fax number are e-mailed to you as a PDF file, so you can view them on your computer screen and print them out only if you need to. And faxes you wish to send can be uploaded from your computer and sent either to another virtual fax machine or to a conventional one.

Save $$: Up to $100 on fax machine purchase price and up to $200 per year on telecommunications and paper and ink costs.

Save the Planet: Conserve the resources used to make the fax machine, the environmental cost of disposal, and the paper used to receive faxes—most of which are likely junk faxes.

Good for You: Receive faxes anywhere you have access to a computer. If you travel for business, you won't miss an important fax. Virtual faxes also protect confidential information from being seen by other people in your office.

OFFICE SUPPLIES

Second Time Around

The SHIFT: Buy 100% postconsumer recycled paper for printers and copiers.

Even $$: Prices can be comparable.

Save the Planet: For an office that uses two cases of paper per month, using recycled paper saves a total of 14 trees, 4,200 gallons of water, and 36 pounds of air pollution.

Good for You: Contrary to what many people believe, recycled paper is not brown or pulpy. In fact, it's much easier to make new paper from old paper than it is to make new paper from wood. Furthermore, the weight and brightness of postconsumer recycled paper is equal to that of virgin paper.

SWIFT SHIFT: GO BIG!

We purchase all our supplies in bulk in order to cut back on packaging and resources. We choose 100% recycled materials when possible, and we buy solid ink instead of cartridges for our copiers and printers. These shifts alone have saved our two offices almost $2,500 per year.

Brooke, New York City
Founder and Owner of a Creative Services Management Agency

Toner Up

The SHIFT: Recycle toner cartridges. When your copier or printer toner cartridge runs dry, take it to an office supply store or toner buyback company so it can be refilled or recycled.

Save $$: Up to $150 per year depending on printing frequency and cartridge brand and model.

Save the Planet: Recycling toner cartridges allows them to be remanufactured or refilled, which not only keeps them out of landfills but also conserves the resources that would have otherwise been used to make brand-new cartridges.

Good for You: Some nonprofit organizations collect empty toner cartridges in their fund-raising efforts. Many organizations will accept your spent cartridges and provide you the mail-back materials free of charge.

Both Sides Now

The SHIFT: Before you toss it in the recycling bin, use the backside of printed paper as scratch paper for taking notes or printing drafts of documents.

Save $$: Up to $250 per year if the average worker in an office of 25 employees reused five sheets of scrap copy paper per day instead of using new sheets.

Save the Planet: Save more than 31,000 sheets of paper per year, and almost 4 trees.

Good for You: Using both sides of a sheet of paper is one of those small shifts of habit that puts you in the mind-set to make bigger ones. It's a change that's easy to commit to—and every time you do it you're reinforcing the idea of yourself as someone who consumes consciously.

Read the Fine Print

The SHIFT: Print only the pages you need. Reformat documents in order to use the fewest sheets of paper possible.

Save $$: Up to $1,600 per year on the cost of paper and printer ink if everyone in a 25-person company printed ten fewer sheets per day.

Save the Planet: Save more than 60,000 sheets of paper per year for the average company as well as roughly 25 printer cartridges.

THE PAPER CHASE: HOW TO USE LESS PAPER (AND BARELY EVEN NOTICE)

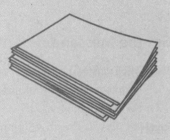

- Narrow the margin settings on your word-processing program.
- Choose a smaller font size.
- Print two pages side-by-side on one sheet of paper.
- Print double-sided sheets. (Some newer printers offer this as a default option.)
- Try single or 1.5 line spacing instead of double spacing.
- Don't print cover sheets, title pages, or appendices until your document is final and ready for distribution.
- When printing e-mails or web pages, use the "print preview" option and print only the pages that contain the information you need.
- Deliver documents electronically, or post them to a website or blog.
- When multiple co-workers are collaborating on a project, post documents to an online file management site. This allows specified users to read, make changes, and offer comments. The best part is that everyone works on the same version of the file simultaneously, so multiple versions don't generate confusion and inefficiency.

Double Duty

The SHIFT: Set the copier's default setting to print double-sided copies.

Save $$: Up to $500 per year in copy paper costs for an office with 25 employees.

Save the Planet: Save 60,000 sheets of paper per year, seven trees, and the energy, water, and pollution associated with paper manufacturing.

Good for You: Save time reloading the paper tray, as well as file space for storing documents and storage space for keeping spare cases of paper.

Get the Message

The SHIFT: Instead of passing out paper memos about an upcoming meeting, event, or announcement, just send the information through e-mail.

Save $$: An office with 25 employees that cuts back on just four memos per week could save $80 per year in paper and ink costs.

Save the Planet: Save 5,000 sheets of paper per year and two printer cartridges.

Good for You: Keep memos from cluttering up your desk, getting lost, or being inadvertently thrown away. Gain instant access to them on your computer.

BREAKROOM

Wash Your Cup

The SHIFT: Use ceramic coffee mugs instead of taking a new paper or foam cup every morning—and afternoon—for hot beverages at work.

Save $$: Up to $2,000 per year for a company of 25 employees where each worker uses an average of two disposable cups per day.

Save the Planet: Keep 12,500 foam or paper cups and plastic lids out of the waste stream.

Good for You: Unlike Styrofoam or plastic-coated cups, you can safely reheat a ceramic mug of coffee or tea in the microwave.

SWIFT SHIFT: CLEANING UP THE KITCHEN

I've never been a fan of plastic bottles, so we use a low-energy water cooler that filters water from the tap. This is saving us $1,500 per year compared with what most small offices spend on bottled water delivery. The extra money in our budget more than offsets the additional costs incurred when we order food for company events. I'm a believer in supporting businesses that provide local, organic, and unprocessed food. To reduce waste, we use real plates, cups, and silverware instead of plastic. And all of our coffee is Fair Trade Certified.

Brooke, New York City
Founder and Owner of a Creative Services Management Agency

Get Your Filter

The SHIFT: Use a water filter pitcher (or faucet attachment) and reusable cups instead of buying individual water bottles or subscribing to a water cooler delivery service.

Save $$: Up to $2,500 or more per year on bottled water costs for a company of 25 employees.

Save the Planet: Keep plastic bottles out of the waste stream, and save the fossil fuel energy used to manufacture and transport the product.

Good for You: As I've mentioned before, municipal water is regulated and bottled water is not.

Shift-it Tip: If you count on the hot water dispenser on the water cooler for making tea and hot cocoa, just have an electric teakettle available to employees instead. It'll have your water boiling in minutes.

Sweet and Low

The SHIFT: Buy cream and sugar in bulk instead of in single-serving packets.

Save $$: Up to $125 per year on condiment costs.

Save the Planet: Reduce packaging waste.

Good for You: Use as much or as little as you want—don't let a pre-measured serving dictate it for you. And buying cream and sugar at the grocery store instead of from a distributor offers more variety.

Recycled Napkins

The SHIFT: If it's not reasonable to designate a personalized cloth napkin to each employee, buy paper napkins made with recycled content.

Even $$: Prices can be comparable with conventional napkins.

Save the Planet: Save tree resources, energy, water, and chemicals (it takes a lot of chemicals to turn wood pulp into something as soft as a napkin). You'll also reduce waste—perhaps even enough to save you money on garbage costs.

SWIFT SHIFT: LADIES AND GENTLEMEN WHO LUNCH

Once we started shifting, we began to see that throwing away Baggies and aluminum foil, drinking out of disposable water bottles, and buying individual servings of anything instead of portioning it out ourselves was really wasteful. So we made the shift to pack trash-free lunches—not just for the kids but for ourselves as well.

Melissa gets positive comments on the reusable wrap she packs our sandwiches in. She feels like she gets to "market" them to her friends, and is planning to buy a few and give them away as gifts. Maybe it's a gender thing, because I get teased for mine.

The guys at work made fun of me for my wife packing my lunch in my son's Pokémon backpack. When I explained what we were doing, they said, "What's up with that hippie stuff?" But with the $600 we're saving a year and the conscience we're developing in our children, I don't mind it a bit. They're probably just jealous.

Michael, Huntsville, AL
Biomedical Technician
Married, Father of Zoë, 12; Jackson, 5; and Cole, 4

Fork Lift

The SHIFT: Instead of buying plastic utensils, buy ones that are compostable—derived from corn, potato, or another renewable starch. Better yet, have actual silverware available to employees in the breakroom, which they can wash when they're finished using them.

Save $$: Pricing can be comparable.

Save the Planet: Conserve petroleum resources and, if compostable utensils are tossed in with the green waste, reduce waste sent to the landfill.

Good for You: Compostable utensils are usually sturdier than the inexpensive plastic variety, so they're less likely to break and more likely to be reused. They also feel strangely good in your mouth, and have smooth, rather than sharp, edges. No more tiny cuts on the corners of your mouth post-yogurt!

COMMUNITY

The Power Hour

The SHIFT: Meet co-workers for happy hour instead of going out for a full dinner.

Save $$: If happy hour means discounted—or free—appetizers and drinks, you could save $25 or more compared with what you'd spend on dinner. If you did this once a week instead of going out to dinner, you'll see a savings of $1,250 per year.

Save the Planet: Going out for appetizers usually means you eat less overall, which typically means less energy and resources were used to produce and cook the food you order. You're also less likely to need takeout containers when things are shared, since somebody's bound to finish them.

Good for You: If you can restrain yourself from gorging on specialty cocktails and wings, sticking instead to the house red (for the antioxidants) and vegetable- and seafood-based appetizers, you'll feel more virtuous than if you'd gone out for meat and potatoes.

Take a Walk

The SHIFT: Start a walking club. Take part of your lunch break or some time after work to go walking with co-workers. If you work in a progressive environment, you may even be able to take a brainstorming session or meeting outside.

Save $$: Taking a walk instead of pay-as-you-go exercise classes could save you $10–$20 per day—more than $1,000 per year if you go twice a week.

Save the Planet: Better health means you spend less energy and fewer resources driving to doctors' offices, taking synthetic prescription drugs, and undergoing tests and procedures.

Good for You: If you walk outside during the day, you can get your daily dose of vitamin D and also get your blood moving to feel energized for the second half of your workday, making you more productive and satisfied with your job. Perhaps most important, new research has shown that regular exercise helps the body produce hormones that reduce stress and promote health, lowering risks of heart disease and cancer. Not to mention that walking daily—especially uphill!—will lead to a great improvement in the appearance of your bottom.

COMMUTING

For more on the best ways to get to work, check out the Transportation and Travel chapter, on page 223.

Meet Me in Cyberspace

The SHIFT: Arrange virtual meetings. Save time and gas by holding a conference call or videoconference instead of traveling to an in-person meeting.

Save $$: Up to $6,000 per year or more if one overnight business trip is eliminated per month (actual savings varies depending on distance, mode of travel, and other expenses such as hotel, taxis, and food).

Save the Planet: Save transport fuel and reduce greenhouse gas emissions. Conserve energy and water by avoiding hotel rooms and restaurants.

Good for You: Save time traveling, avoid traffic and airport delays, and sleep better in your own bed—in your own time zone.

SWIFT SHIFT: IT'S NOT WHERE YOU'RE GOING, IT'S HOW YOU GET THERE

It's amazing how many of my employees ride their bikes, walk, or take the subway to work. My own New York apartment isn't far from the office. I designed my life that way, so I could walk everywhere. It wouldn't make sense to rent an apartment on the other side of the city from where I work. I want to keep my life simple.

Brooke, New York City
Founder and Owner of a Creative Services Management Agency

CONTINUING EDUCATION

A Virtual Genius!

The SHIFT: If you're thinking of enrolling in a class or two as a way to improve your skills or switch careers, consider taking them online.

Save $$: Up to $240 on gas costs compared with driving 20 miles round-trip to school twice a week.

Save the Planet: Reduce gas consumption by up to 60 gallons or more.

> ### COURSE THE WEB
> Nearly 4 million students enrolled in online classes in 2008. Many universities offer them as alternatives to classroom courses. And they're just as rigorous.

Good for You: Time is the huge benefit here. If you're learning from home, you'll not only save about an hour a day or more of driving time, but you'll save the time you'd spend finding a parking spot and walking to and from class, and the time you take to get ready. Who says you can't take classes online in your pajamas?

WORK: The Bottom Line

Make these shifts and your company could save **$30,000** or more annually! As an employee—or even if you just have a home office—these shifts could save you more than **$4,100** per year!

For additional ideas about everything from recycled office products to how to activate your computer's power management system, check out **http://shiftyourhabit.com**.

MEET THE SHIFTERS:
Samantha, Rob, Allison, and Kellie

Samantha and Rob have two girls: Allison is fifteen years old and Kellie is age nine. Rob manages a home-improvement store, and Samantha works at a health insurance company. Samantha wants to steer her family away from conspicuous consumption, and toward spending more creative time together.

Coming into this project, I cared about the environment in a passive don't-throw-trash-out-of-a-car-window kind of way. I would recycle whenever a bin was nearby but not when it was inconvenient. I turned off lights most of the time and drove a smaller car. In retrospect, though, I suppose my friend Shannon was right when she called my family "environmentally challenged." We weren't making a direct connection between our actions and the state of our planet.

When Elizabeth sent us our first set of family shifts, I think I was expecting them to involve a complete overhaul of our way of life. I thought I'd see instructions on how to build a composter or how to pedal a bike to power my dishwasher! But I was pleasantly surprised that all of

Elizabeth's suggestions were really doable. My nine-year-old daughter was excited and jumped in wholeheartedly. My fifteen-year-old daughter was mildly interested (as much as you can expect from a teenage girl!). And my husband was a little hesitant and nervous—what had his wife gotten him into now?

This whole experience has felt like a really good spring cleaning—of our home, our bodies, and our way of thinking. I've noticed that the environment has actually become a topic of conversation in my family, which it never was before. It really shook up our home a bit!

The other day I ran into my friend Shannon at my daughter's softball practice. She's the one who used to refer to me as environmentally challenged. Anyway, she noticed the bag I was using to carry equipment and told me how cute it was. I told her it was made from 100% recycled materials. "Who are you?" she asked me. And it dawned on me then that we've really opened our minds, embraced this new green lifestyle, and changed for the better.

Samantha, Orange County, CA
Insurance Company Project Manager
Married, Mother of Allison, 15, and Kellie, 9

ELECTRONICS and ENTERTAINMENT

We live in a disposable society. It's no small challenge, for example, to keep the same cell phone for more than a year, especially when it's been designed to self-destruct as soon as a newer model appears. In many ways, electronics have become more ephemeral than fashion trends. It's simply more cost-effective to buy a new phone than to have a broken one repaired. The last time I took my laptop to be serviced, the sales associate looked at me as though I had three heads. *Why didn't I just buy a new one already?* One word, my friends: e-waste.

E-waste is the term used to describe the millions and millions of tons of abandoned electronics we throw away every year. While some decays in landfills, more and more e-waste is being exported to developing countries in Asia and Africa to be "recycled" by poor people—many of whom are children. The dirty job of disassembling our rejected electronics in order to remove the valuable and reusable components results in workers' exposure to disease-causing toxins as well as in environmental damage from heavy metals and hazardous material contamination. So I do everything I can to prolong the life of my stuff in order to keep it from contributing to the growth of such a repulsive industry.

Now, I'm not antitechnology. Even though their production and functioning require energy and involve less-than-earth-friendly materials, many gadgets actually enable us to be more green. I say *enable* instead of *compel,* though, because in order for computers and cell phones to help conserve resources, we have to take advantage of all the benefits they offer. Unfortunately, most of us don't.

Take digital cameras, for example. They allow us to shoot and store our photos digitally, eliminating the need for paper and ink. But instead of looking at them online, many of us print digital photos anyway. Broadband Internet access means we can stream movies directly to our computers, eliminating the need for cable service and DVDs. Yet most of us pay for cable (or satellite) and DVDs anyway. Downloadable music and software have, for the most part, eliminated the need to buy physical CDs. Still, we often find ourselves at the checkout counter purchasing the new release of a long-awaited album or the latest version of our favorite computer program (both of which are drowned in packaging, I might add).

The future of technology will depend on its ability to truly enhance the quality of human life. In my mind, machines and gadgets are at their best when they help us connect with one another, or streamline once-arduous tasks so we can spend more time away from our gadgets and in the moments that really matter.

In this chapter, you'll discover ways for you and your family to make those machines work for you—not the other way around.

TELEVISION

Hide the Clicker

The SHIFT: It may sound drastic, but more and more households are living without television. Wanna give it a try?

Save $$: About $1,000 per year on satellite or cable bills and energy costs.

Save the Planet: Reduce energy consumption by about 1,000 kilowatt-hours per year.

Shift-it Tip: Now that you'll have an additional four hours per day to spend as you wish, you can read for pleasure, discover a new hobby, exercise more, spend quality time with your family, volunteer in your community—or just get a little more sleep.

TUBIN'

The average television viewer watches 140–150 hours of TV per month, which adds up to nearly 1,800 hours per year.

The U.S. Environmental Protection Agency estimates that Americans spend nearly $8 billion per year in energy costs to run their television sets.

SWIFT SHIFT: CUT THE CABLE

Even though we used to love to veg out in front of the TV to relax, we've chosen to give up cable and watch DVDs instead. We're not only saving a lot of money—more than $750 per year—but we're finally taking control of our TV-watching schedule. We now have to make a conscious decision to watch a movie instead of mindlessly flopping down in front of the tube whenever we have free time.

Jill and Jeremy, Orlando, FL
Medical Administrator and Realtor
Pet Lovers and Parents-to-Be

Turn Your Computer into a TV

The SHIFT: Cancel your cable service and watch TV shows online through the network websites. It's free and totally legal.

Save $$: Up to $900 per year on your cable or satellite bill.

Save the Planet: Computers use far less energy than the typical television entertainment system, so you'll be saving energy and reducing greenhouse gas emissions as well.

Shift-it Tip: Being intentional about the shows you watch will help you to manage your time more efficiently and not get sucked into staring at the glowing box regardless of what's on.

Special Delivery

The SHIFT: Rent movie downloads or use a mailbox delivery service instead of driving to your nearest video store.

Save $$: Up to $450 per year if you rent, on average, three movies per weekend.

Save the Planet: Spare the gasoline it takes to pick up and drop off movies from the rental store. Movies rented online are either delivered with your mail—which doesn't take much additional fuel—or streamed directly to your computer.

Shift-it Tip: If you're a movie buff, renting online can be an efficient and economical way to stay up-to-date on the latest releases.

Strip Club

The SHIFT: Instead of leaving your television, DVD player, satellite receiver, audio equipment, and video game console in standby mode when they're not in use, make turning them off easy on yourself by plugging into a power strip. Just flip the power strip off when you go to bed at night. Better yet, buy a power strip with a timer that you can program to shut off automatically.

Save $$: Up to $50 on electricity bills per year running electronics you're not actively using!

Save the Planet: Conserve almost 500 kilowatt-hours of energy per year.

SWIFT SHIFT: DON'T FLY STANDBY

Our family loves music and movies. And like most American families, we probably watch too much television. In all, we have 18 pieces of entertainment equipment—from TVs to satellite receivers to DVD players to sound systems. I estimate that each is on for about 6 hours per day. When Elizabeth asked us whether any were plugged in to power strips, I replied that they weren't. What did it matter since they were turned off when they weren't being used? Then I learned about standby power—the energy electronics continue to draw even when they're powered off. Now that we're using power strips to turn off our entertainment systems, we're going to be saving close to $60 per year on energy that we had been wasting.

Samantha, Orange County, CA
Insurance Company Project Manager
Married, Mother of Allison, 15, and Kellie, 9

Boycott the Plasma Drive

The SHIFT: If you're in the market for a new TV, choose a rear projection or liquid crystal display (LCD) flat screen over a plasma television. Of your television options, plasma TVs typically consume about 50% more energy than LCD or rear-projection televisions.

Save $$: Up to $40 per year in electricity costs.

Save the Planet: Conserve roughly 400 kilowatt-hours of electricity per year—nearly as much as you'd save by leaving your TV turned off for more than six months.

Good for You: You may save additional money during the summer on AC bills, as plasma screens generate significantly more heat than LCD or rear projection systems.

Tube Together

The SHIFT: Instead of each person in your household watching his or her own television in a separate room, why not watch TV together?

Save $$: Up to $35 per year if watching shows together can eliminate an average of 4 total hours of television time per day.

Save the Planet: Reduce energy consumption by 350 kilowatt-hours per year and keep 400 pounds of greenhouse gases out of the atmosphere.

Shift-it Tip: While it may not be as effective as eating dinner together or sharing an evening stroll, watching television with your friends or family can be a low-stress way to bond—especially if you're watching a show that you look forward to discussing each week.

Background Noise

The SHIFT: The average household's television is turned on for more than 8 hours per day, but the average person watches TV for only 4.5 hours daily. That's 3.5 hours of unwatched TV cluttering up your family's consciousness. Why not turn it off and do something else?

Save $$: Up to $30 per year or more depending on the type and size of the TV you own.

Save the Planet: Save nearly 300 kilowatt-hours of electricity and reduce greenhouse gas emissions by 350 pounds per year.

Flat Out?

Are flat-screen TVs better or worse for the environment than the old big ones?

The most eco-friendly television set is the one you already own. There's no point in getting a new TV for the purpose of saving energy. The cost to the environment of disposing of your old set and providing the resources needed to make a new one far outweigh any energy differences you might see between one TV and another.

Now, if you're in the market for a new television and energy efficiency is important to you, here's a breakdown of television energy costs, according to the EPA:

TV Model	Average Annual Energy Use	Average Annual Energy Use
Cathode Ray Tube (CRT)	244 kWh	$27
Liquid Crystal Display (LCD)	256 kWh	$28
Plasma	679 kWh	$75

Before you buy, look into the power consumption of the television you're considering. And especially check its standby power rating. In some televisions, the energy consumed during standby can be nearly as much as the energy consumed while the unit is active. Buying an ENERGY STAR qualified model is always best.

Bright Idea

The SHIFT: Since most televisions are calibrated to have a very bright picture, reducing your TV's light output can save you significant energy.

Save $$: Up to $15 per year.

Save the Planet: Conserve 150 kilowatt-hours per year, which is enough to power a 42-inch flat-screen TV nonstop for 30 straight days.

Stop the Quick Start

The SHIFT: Turn off the Quick Start option on your HDTV.

Save $$: Up to $5 per year on electricity bills.

Save the Planet: Save 60 kilowatt-hours of energy per year.

Shift-it Tip: Although Quick Start may help your television fire up a bit faster, it consumes up to fifty times more energy when in standby mode.

MOVIES

Screening Room

The SHIFT: Instead of driving to the theater for a show on the big screen, watch a movie in the comfort of your own living room.

Save $$: Up to $230 if you make this shift, on average, for one movie per month.

Save the Planet: Your environmental impact is lowest if you use a mail-order movie rental service, as you'll avoid burning the fuel used to drive to the theater or video rental store.

Good for You: In addition to being able to pause the movie if nature calls—or rewind it if you missed something—you'll eliminate the temptations posed by overpriced, overbuttered movie popcorn, candy, sodas, and other less-than-healthful snacks.

Pop Art

The SHIFT: Share a single bag of popcorn with your movie dates instead of getting multiple small bags.

Save $$: Up to $50 on popcorn costs if you eliminate one quart-size bag per month.

Save the Planet: Reduce the waste and energy associated with popcorn production, packaging, and disposal.

Shift-it Tip: If you share a small popcorn, you'll eat less overall and avoid that sick feeling of eating way too much on an empty stomach.

POP(CORN) CULTURE

Americans consume an average of 54 quarts of popcorn per man, woman, and child. Of this, about 16 quarts are consumed away from home, at places like movie theaters and ballparks. One small bag of movie popcorn has 400 calories and 27 grams of fat.

News Flash

The SHIFT: Instead of subscribing to a newspaper or buying a paper from a newsstand, read your news online.

Save $$: Up to $350 per year on a newspaper subscription.

Save the Planet: Reduce consumption by 700 pounds of paper and about six trees. Although newsprint is made with some recycled content, only about half of all newspapers are recycled. This means virgin paper—from trees—must still be used to create fresh newsprint.

Shift-it Tip: Most newspapers offer news for free on their websites. Online news is updated almost instantaneously, so you won't have to wait until tomorrow to learn about today's happenings.

ALL THE NEWS (NOT) FIT TO PRINT

In 1998 just 13% of Americans got their news from an online source. A decade later, the percentage had nearly tripled to 37%.

MUSIC

Get Down with the Download

The SHIFT: Purchase and download music from the Internet instead of buying CDs.

Save $$: Up to $300 per year if you buy three albums per month.

Save the Planet: Conserve the resources that go into manufacturing CDs and their cases as well as the environmental costs of disposal that are incurred when they eventually break or become obsolete.

Shift-it Tip: Music downloads allow you to pick and choose the songs you want to hear, so you'll no longer find yourself having wasted money on a 14-song CD with only a single hit. Music downloads also make it easy to create themed playlists for special events or activities.

SWIFT SHIFT: COMPACT DISS

We have recently started downloading music instead of buying CDs. The best part for me is the convenience of being able to buy only the songs I like instead of being stuck with stacks of CDs containing songs I don't care for—especially since we're running out of space to store all of those jewel cases. I figure with our penchant for music, downloads will save us about $300 or more a year.

Samantha, Orange County, CA
Insurance Company Project Manager
Married, Mother of Allison, 15, and Kellie, 9

Open Pandora's Box

The SHIFT: Don't want to spend the money to buy your favorite tunes? Check out Pandora.com, Rhapsody.com, the iTunes Genius feature, or a similar online music provider. Enter the name of a song or artist that suits your fancy and the provider will put together a stream of music that fits your taste, including the artists you like and others similar to them.

Save $$: Up to $140 per year compared with subscribing to satellite radio or to buying ten CDs per year.

> **DISKPOSAL**
>
> An estimated two billion CDs have been discarded and taken to landfills per year since 2005.

Save the Planet: If you've got a computer—or even a web-connected phone—you don't need to buy any additional equipment to listen to Internet radio.

Shift-it Tip: Get exposed to music you might not otherwise have heard of. There's no risk involved since you're not spending any money. If you don't like a song, just "tell" the website and you'll never have to hear it again.

Recharge Your Batteries

The SHIFT: If you frequently use a portable radio, digital camera, handheld flashlight, or recording device, chances are you go through new batteries about once a month. Instead, invest in some rechargeable ones.

Save $$: Up to $60 per year or more on battery costs.

Save the Planet: Reduce battery waste, which can be a source of contamination when batteries are disposed of improperly (that is, in the garbage).

Good for You: No need to jump in the car to buy new batteries if yours go dead. Just recharge for a few hours and they're good as new.

Shift-it Tip: Whether they're single-use or rechargeable, take dead batteries to a battery recycling center instead of throwing them away. Check out http://earth911.com for the location nearest you.

Dollars and Incentives

The SHIFT: Before you consider tossing or e-cycling your broken or obsolete gadgets, check to see if any local electronics or office supply stores are offering incentives to take them off your hands.

Save $$: Depending on the incentive, you may get store credit, a percentage discount off a new model, or a cash rebate.

Save the Planet: Recycling electronics properly makes it possible for their components to be reused, remanufactured, or disposed of in a manner that causes minimal damage to people or the environment.

What to Do with Your E-Waste

Just the idea of disposing of pounds and pounds of outdated plastic and microchips is daunting. That's why so many of us end up letting old computers gather dust in our storage rooms, or send them out with the trash.

Here's what to ask yourself if your machines have seen better days. First, is your device still working? If yes, ask yourself whether you really need a new one. Once you've thoroughly thought through the idea of a new purchase, donate your old device, or sell it through eBay or craigslist. If your device isn't working, get a repair estimate—it may be worth fixing.

If you must dispose of your used electronics, seek out a responsible e-cycler by visiting www.e-stewards.org, or ask existing recyclers about their e-cycling processes.

E-cyclers certified by the e-Stewards organization have made the following commitments to social and environmental responsibility:

- No exporting of e-waste to developing countries
- No disposal of toxins in landfills or incinerators
- Tracking of toxins throughout the disposal process
- Worker health and safety
- No disassembly and processing procedures that may lead to environmental contamination by heavy metals and other toxins
- No diverting of e-waste processing to prisons
- High standards for electronic components designated for reuse

PHONE

For Old Phone's Sake

The SHIFT: Just because your cell phone service provider offers you a great deal on a new phone every 18 months doesn't mean you have to take the company up on it. Keep your cell phone for three years or more instead.

Save $$: Up to $36 on activation fees per phone—and up to $200 on the phone itself. If you were planning to upgrade to a phone with more features that require more bandwidth—such as Internet access, e-mail, and GPS—you could save an additional $500 per year on your cell plan by staying low-fi.

Save the Planet: Save the resources used to make new phones as well as the environmental impacts of cell phone disposal. More than 150 million cell phones are replaced every year, and most are still in working order when they're retired.

BUYING A NEW PHONE

If you're in the market for a new phone, look for the following features:

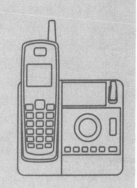

- Easily recyclable
- Made from recycled parts
- Meets EU standards (more stringent than U.S. standards) for toxic substances
- Free of lead, cadmium, and mercury
- ENERGY STAR qualified chargers

PHOTOS

Show and Tell

The SHIFT: Use an online photo-sharing site to show off your newest pics to friends and family instead of printing them out.

Save $$: Up to $60 per year if you take an average of 30 pictures per month.

Save the Planet: Save the paper, chemical inks and dyes, and energy required to print digital photos.

Good for You: Keeping your photos in digital form, on either a hard drive or a CD, makes their storage and transport much easier and more practical than having shelves full of picture albums. They're also less likely to get lost or destroyed.

> **WITHOUT LEAVING A FILM**
>
> When it comes to taking pictures, we're all going digital. In 2008, 75% of U.S. households owned at least one digital camera, up from 31% in 2004 and just 4.4% in 1999.

SWIFT SHIFT: SCRAP THE SCRAPBOOK

I am a HUGE picture taker! I am a former and still-wanna-be scrapbooker, so I have boxes and boxes (and boxes!) of pictures and mementos shoved into an extra closet. Since buying a digital camera, I'm now using an online photo site to upload, share, and print my pictures. I'm probably saving $300–$400 per year on printing costs, not to mention all of the photo paper and chemicals that were used to develop double prints of my film—and of course all of the trash created when I'd have to throw away two of every picture that didn't come out. What a waste that was!

Samantha, Orange County, CA
Insurance Company Project Manager
Married, Mother of Allison, 15, and Kellie, 9

EVENTS, MUSEUMS, and AMUSEMENT PARKS

Join the Club

The SHIFT: For the cost of two or three general admission tickets to a museum, you can become a member and get unlimited family admission for the entire year. Most museums display traveling exhibits, so you can see something new each time you visit.

Save $$: Up to $360 per year compared with buying two $15 event tickets per month. As a bonus, most museum memberships are tax deductible.

Save the Planet: Membership at a local park or museum means you'll save the fuel you'd spend to drive to an event farther away.

Good for You: Explore new works of art, engage your mind, experience culture, and become part of the arts community in your area.

Watering Hole

The SHIFT: Whether you're at an amusement park, ball game, or county fair, don't waste money on overpriced bottles of water. Instead, bring your own bottle and refill it at the drinking fountains.

Save $$: Up to $20 for a family of four per event.

Save the Planet: Reduce bottle waste and conserve the fossil fuel resources used to produce and transport the plastic.

Good for You: More budget left for things you can't bring with you, like hot dogs and ice cream.

Prize Winner

The SHIFT: Who needs a life-size stuffed dog or a purse full of cheap plastic trinkets? Play a carnival game whose prize you might actually find useful—not one that will sit and gather dust for a year and then get tossed out with the garbage.

Save $$: Up to $25 or more if you choose to forgo carnival games.

Save the Planet: Conserve the energy, materials, and other resources used to produce and transport the winnable prizes. Eventually avoid the waste they generate when they're disposed of (which, in my experience, is soon after they're won).

Shift-it Tip: If you do find yourself carting home a prize from the fair, donate it to a school or charity when you're finished with it instead of throwing it away.

Bag Lunch

The SHIFT: If you choose to buy food at the theater, ball game, fair, or amusement park, opt for vegetarian options and items with little or no packaging.

Save $$: Up to $20 or more for a family of four compared with meat entrees and packaged snacks.

Save the Planet: Conserve resources like land, water, and energy used to raise, process, and package meat, as well as the greenhouse gases associated with raising livestock.

Good for You: Vegetarian items can offer fewer calories and more nutrients than many meaty choices, especially if the meat is mostly fat and preservatives.

Shift-it Tip: Here are some ideas of what to munch on at public events: soft pretzels, falafel sandwiches, french fries, churros, fruit-and-yogurt parfaits, popcorn, Popsicles, and fresh fruit drinks (especially those served inside the fruit itself).

VIDEO GAMES

See page 105 of the Kids chapter.

COMPUTERS and OFFICE EQUIPMENT

See page 152 of the Work chapter.

ELECTRONICS and ENTERTAINMENT: The Bottom Line

Make these shifts and save up to **$3,200** or more!

For the newest green gadgets and ways to run them efficiently, check out **http://shiftyourhabit.com.**

MEET THE SHIFTER:
Christin

Christin, a single twenty-eight-year-old, lives with four roommates in an old apartment in Glendale, California. She is a trained musician and worked as an associate story producer for reality TV until the economic downturn left her unemployed.

Shortly before I met Elizabeth, I had been let go from my job, and no one was hiring story producers for reality TV—my chosen field. After a while I began wondering if I would ever work again. The day I decided to become a part of Shift Your Habit I thought, here's a great way to be a part of something that actually matters. I was excited but also worried that I might let myself down if I failed. I knew I cared about the environment—because obviously, without it, I would cease to exist!—but I had no idea if my actions really matched my beliefs, because I never knew how to accurately assess my carbon footprint. I had a good feeling that being part of this project would be worthwhile.

Some of the ideas seemed crazy and hard to wrap my mind around at first, but once I started doing them, they made sense. When I figured out the strategy behind the shifts, my creative juices went wild. I was shifting everything I could think of. Shift Your Habit allowed me to look at my whole life with a fresh perspective—while having no shortage of laughs in the process.

Ever since I started shifting, I feel like my mind has gotten sharper. My idea lists have tripled. I am taking responsibility for my actions, and am finding new uses for what I already own instead of buying more stuff. I have definitely been suffering financially during this economic meltdown, but the shifts I've made have made a huge difference in offsetting some of my lost income. Still, I wouldn't trade the progress I've made through it for anything!

Christin, Glendale, CA
Single, 28
Television Producer and Vintage Clothing Entrepreneur

HEALTH, BEAUTY, and FASHION

7

This probably won't come as much of a surprise, but when it comes to topics like diet, exercise, fashion, and beauty, I'm a huge believer in simplicity. Eating right and being physically active shouldn't seem like a chore. And dressing well and maintaining a youthful look should never send us deep into debt.

There are hundreds of ideas in this book that can improve the way you look and feel without you even being conscious of it. You're burning calories while tending to your backyard garden; you're giving your lungs a break when you toss those toxic cleaners. Vegetarian meals often contain more nutrition, and are easier to digest, than meaty ones. And that Sunday bike ride with the family is helping everyone build strong bones and muscles.

Yet many of us behave as though looking and feeling good requires running marathons, subsisting on a lifelong crash diet, taking an hour each night to douse our faces in a dozen age-defying chemicals, and spending far more than we can afford on clothes and accessories that will be out of style within a year. Deep down, don't we all know that none of this is sustainable and, even more important, that it's unlikely to make us happy?

The way you look to the world has everything to do with how you feel—your health, your happiness, your self-image. The shifts in this chapter are aimed at boosting your radiance and confidence, in the hopes that everything else will take care of itself.

HEALTH

Check In

The SHIFT: Whether or not you have health insurance, it's important to get an annual checkup to ensure that your body is functioning properly and that you're getting adequate exercise and nutrition.

Save $$: Potentially thousands of dollars on health costs over the long run.

Save the Planet: Reduce the amount of resources and waste consumed over your lifetime for treatment of illnesses that could have been prevented through regular visits to the physician.

Good for You: Some employers and health insurance companies will actually pay you to get a physical—up to $500 per year. Their rationale is that if you're healthy today, you'll save them money in the long run. Regular physicals significantly increase the chance that any serious physical impairments or illnesses will be caught early, reducing the length and intensity of treatment, and perhaps even extending your life.

Don't Be a Pill

The SHIFT: The next time you come down with a cold or flulike symptoms, avoid the temptation to take antibiotics immediately. Instead, get plenty of rest, drink fluids, and if appropriate, use over-the-counter medication for relief.

Save $$: Up to $15 on prescription antibiotics—or more if you don't have insurance.

Save the Planet: The production and disposal of antibiotics consumes resources and leads to the disruption of ecosystems when antibacterial drugs get into water systems and kill off important species of microbes and algae that keep a body of water healthy.

Good for You: The common cold and most strains of flu are viral infections. Antibiotics will do nothing for them. Plus, the widespread use of antibiotics for nonbacterial infections leads to antibiotic resistance, which renders antibiotics ineffective against some common bacteria.

Just Enough of a Good Thing

The SHIFT: Buy a multivitamin instead of a bunch of single vitamin and mineral supplements.

Save $$: Up to $350 per year.

Save the Planet: Conserve the production energy used to generate additional supplements and containers, and significantly reduce your accumulation and disposal of plastic pill bottles and packaging.

Good for You: Let the experts do the work for you—multivitamins contain everything you need. Unless recommended by a health professional, additional supplements may not provide any benefits to your well-being and could cause harm if taken improperly.

Hold Water

The SHIFT: Instead of grabbing a diet soda, iced tea, coffee, or bottle of flavored vitamin water the next time you feel parched, drink what's freely available from the tap.

Save $$: Up to $200 per year.

Save the Planet: Conserve manufacturing and transportation energy and reduce packaging waste from bottles and cans.

Shift-it Tip: Staying hydrated by drinking the proper amount of water is one of the least expensive ways to prevent illness and keep your weight under control. Doctors recommend that people drink half their weight in ounces. So a 150-pound person should drink 75 ounces of liquids per day—or a little less than ten 8-ounce glasses.

FITNESS

Get a Move On

The SHIFT: If you don't exercise regularly, get yourself in shape. Find a walking buddy, join a gym, download online yoga classes, or hit the bike path. Your options are almost limitless!

Save $$: Studies show that physically active individuals pay, on average, about $1,500 less per year in medical costs compared with inactive individuals. Significant health benefits occur with at least 2.5 hours per week of moderately intense activity such as brisk walking. Depending on your age and current physical health condition, your financial savings may not be evident immediately. And, of course, for the sake of your health and safety, a medical doctor should be consulted before you begin any exercise routine.

Save the Planet: Prescription medications, special medical tests, and doctors' visits all have an environmental impact. Medical waste such as needles must be incinerated, which releases greenhouse gases and other pollutants into the atmosphere. Medical equipment is energy and resource intensive to produce, use, and maintain. Finally, doctor and hospital visits involve driving. And chances are, the more severe your health condition, the more trips you'll take and the farther you'll have to drive to see specialists.

Good for You: People who maintain a healthy weight are at lower risk for numerous types of ailments including heart disease, diabetes, high blood pressure, cancer, depression, and osteoporosis. Exercise has been shown to reduce blood pressure, control weight, build healthy muscles, bones, and joints—and even promote happiness.

Vita-Minimum

Rather than downing supplements, eating a well-balanced diet of vitamin-rich foods may serve you better in the long run. Vitamins in food are easier to absorb than supplements—and consuming them is a much better experience. They're also cheaper!

Here's how to chew your daily allowances without resorting to chewables.

If you need . . .	Then eat . . .
Vitamin A	carrots, mangos, apricots, sweet potatoes, spinach, pink grapefruit, tomatoes, collard greens, salmon, shellfish, milk, egg yolks
Vitamin B_1	asparagus, mushrooms, spinach, romaine lettuce, sunflower seeds, green peas, tomatoes, eggplant, brussels sprouts, tuna
Vitamin B_2	mushrooms, spinach, romaine lettuce, asparagus, chard, mustard greens, broccoli, collard greens, turnip greens, venison, eggs, yogurt, cow's milk
Vitamin B_3	mushrooms, asparagus, kelp, seaweed, tuna, beef liver, halibut, venison, chicken, salmon
Vitamin B_6	spinach, bell peppers, turnip greens, garlic, cauliflower, mustard greens, banana, celery, cabbage, mushrooms, asparagus, broccoli, kale, collard greens, brussels sprouts, chard, tuna, cod
Vitamin B_{12}	venison, shrimp, scallops, salmon, beef, milk, cheese, eggs
Vitamin C	broccoli, bell peppers, kale, strawberries, turnip greens, brussels sprouts, papaya, chard, spinach, kiwi, snow peas, cantaloupe, oranges, grapefruit, tomatoes, zucchini, raspberries, asparagus, pineapple
Vitamin D	salmon, shrimp, vitamin-D-fortified milk, cod, eggs, sunlight (best source)

If you need . . .	Then eat . . .
Vitamin E	mustard greens, turnip greens, chard, sunflower seeds, almonds, spinach, collard greens, papaya, olives, bell peppers, brussels sprouts, kiwi, tomatoes, blueberries, broccoli
Vitamin K	spinach, brussels sprouts, chard, green beans, asparagus, broccoli, kale, mustard greens, green peas, carrots
Calcium	spinach, chard, kale, romaine lettuce, celery, broccoli, sesame seeds, summer squash, green beans, garlic, tofu, brussels sprouts, oranges, asparagus, mushrooms, yogurt, mozzarella cheese, cow's milk, goat's milk
Folic Acid	romaine lettuce, spinach, asparagus, broccoli, cauliflower, beets, lentils, squash, black beans, pinto beans, garbanzo beans, papaya, green beans, calf's liver
Iodine	kelp, strawberries, yogurt, cow's milk, eggs, mozzarella cheese
Iron	chard, spinach, romaine lettuce, tofu, mustard greens, turnip greens, green beans, shiitake mushrooms, lentils, brussels sprouts, asparagus, garbanzo beans, broccoli, kelp, beef, venison
Magnesium	chard, spinach, squash, broccoli, blackstrap molasses, turnip greens, cucumber, green beans, celery, kale, sunflower seeds, sesame seeds, flax seeds, halibut
Zinc	mushrooms, spinach, summer squash, asparagus, chard, collard greens, miso, broccoli, peas, sesame seeds, mustard greens, calf's liver, venison, beef, lamb, shrimp, yogurt

SWIFT SHIFT: GOLF PRO

Even though I was living with four roommates when I started this project, I lived on a pretty tight budget. It wasn't uncommon for me to scrounge around for change to buy a couple of 99-cent tacos so I could eat dinner. I had been saving up for several months to be able to pay the startup fee for a gym membership. Now I've ditched that idea altogether for—drum roll, please—Frisbee golf! Frisbee golf is just like golf, but instead of a ball, you use a Frisbee. You should have seen my boyfriend and me trying to get that disk into the metal basket from what seemed a mile away and not hit anyone in the process! It was the best time I'd had in years! The exercise was far better than what I could get on a treadmill, much more entertaining than whatever random news program was showing in the gym's cardio room, and totally free! I'll be saving about $30 per month, which turns out to be just enough to buy an extra taco every day!

Christin, Glendale, CA
Television Producer and Vintage Clothing Entrepreneur
Single, 28

No Equipment Necessary

The SHIFT: Resist the urge to buy a piece of fitness equipment. If you're a walker or jogger, hit the streets and trails around your community. If you're a bike person, get a real bike and ride it to work or around the neighborhood with your kids. Granted, those options don't lend themselves to watching TV or reading a magazine while working out (and may not work in all climates), but they're a lot cheaper and better for the environment.

Save $$: Up to $2,000 on the initial cost of the equipment and $25 per year or more on energy costs (if the equipment has a motor).

Save the Planet: Keep unused machines from eventually clogging up landfills. Surveys show that half of American households own at least one piece of fitness equipment, yet only one in four actually uses that equipment on a regular basis.

Good for You: Unless a doctor's recommendation or extenuating circumstances are leading you to buy an exercise machine, avoid the hassle and the headache of buying, transporting, and assembling something that will probably end up as just a really expensive clothes rack.

SWIFT SHIFT:
THE GYM HAS GONE TO THE DOGS

Since we started shifting, Jill has been walking the dog in the evening to get some exercise. She finally closed her gym membership, which was costing us $130 per year to just keep on hold. Even though at the time it seemed like a reasonable fee, it adds up to quite a bit. After all, that's dinner at a really nice restaurant—or, more practically, a few sets of washable hybrid diapers!

Jeremy, Orlando, FL
Realtor
Married, Pet Lover, and Dad-to-Be

The Band Plays On

The SHIFT: Buy a resistance band exercise system instead of a home weight-lifting gym.

Save $$: Up to $600 or more.

Save the Planet: Save energy from raw material extraction, production, manufacturing, and transport. You'll reduce waste as well, because eventually the monstrous unit will become non-functional, obsolete, or unwanted, and its 200 or more pounds of plastic and metal will end up in a landfill.

Good for You: An average home gym requires 55 square feet of space. Resistance bands can be stored in a drawer.

Bottle Your Enthusiasm

The SHIFT: Bring to the gym a sports bottle that you can reuse and refill instead of buying bottled water or a sports drink from the vending machine.

Save $$: Up to $150 per year if you buy an average of three drink bottles per week.

Save the Planet: Conserve more than 10 pounds of plastic bottle waste as well as the energy and resources used to produce the plastic for the bottles and the fuel to transport them to your gym.

Shift-it Tip: If you're a fan of sports drinks, try making your own by buying the powder form and adding it to your reusable water bottle.

FASHION

Just Donate

The SHIFT: Donate any clothes you don't want that are in good condition to a thrift store or charity.

Save $$: If you itemize your taxes, get a donation receipt from the donation center. For a donation of $500 worth of clothes, you could save $150 or more off your federal taxes the following April.

Save the Planet: Donating unwanted items is one of the best ways to keep them out of the landfill. You'll also help save the water, energy, and land needed to produce raw materials for new clothing.

Shift-it Tip: For people living on a tight budget, thrift-store shopping is an ideal way to fill a wardrobe with often very stylish fashion at very low cost.

SWIFT SHIFT: COTTAGE INDUSTRY

It occurred to me as I was going through my closet one day that I had been holding on to so much vintage clothing. I have boxes and boxes full of cool stuff picked up at thrift stores and yard sales. When I finally put two and two together, I decided to start my own company by applying the shifts method to my business strategy—using what I already have to generate value. My plan is to host private vintage sales in a garden setting. The hidden vintage experience will be an opportunity for people to reduce, reuse, and recycle with style.

Christin, Glendale, CA
Television Producer and Vintage Clothing Entrepreneur
Single, 28

SWIFT SHIFT: MEET CASEY

Casey, a sixteen-year-old junior, was asked to her first high school prom this year. Given a budget of just $100, she was worried she'd have to settle for a less-than-perfect outfit.

I had been stressing so much about what I was going to wear to the prom. Then Elizabeth took me to the same vintage store where she'd bought her own prom dress years ago. It was such an amazing place! There were racks and racks of incredible dresses from the '50s, '60s, '70s, and '80s, and each was one of a kind. I tried on a million dresses but fell in love with a sea blue one with a tiny waist and a full skirt. It cost way less than I would have paid anywhere else, and looked much better. There has never been a better definition for "custom-made." I was so glad to get something I knew no other girl would be wearing. And they told me I looked good enough to grace the cover of a magazine. Can you believe it? Me!

Casey, San Fernando Valley, CA
Daughter, 16, of Nikki

Take Care

The SHIFT: Extend the lifetime of the items in your wardrobe by making an effort to care for them properly.

Save $$: Up to $600 per year if this helps you spend about $50 less per month on clothes overall.

Save the Planet: Conserve the natural resources, energy, and chemical dyes required to manufacture new garments, and also keep old clothes from piling up at the landfill. Unlike clothes that go "out of style"—which, of course, is subjective—stained, ripped, or worn-out clothes are much less likely to be selected by a thrift-store shopper.

Shift-it Tip: Fashion editors have been using this trick for years: If you make a habit of buying new clothes seasonally, limit yourself to just one trendy item and make all your other purchases the highest-quality basics you can afford. True style is not disposable.

HOW TO GIVE YOUR WARDROBE A LONG AND HAPPY LIFE

- Wash like colors together.
- Read the fabric care label before cleaning to prevent garment from shrinking, wrinkling, or being otherwise ruined.
- Hand-wash and line-dry.
- Treat stains immediately.
- Change out of work clothes when you get home to prevent unnecessary wear and tear—and stains—during dinner preparation, housework, baby duty, etc.
- Don't wear clothes you'd go out in to do chores, outdoor work, or activities in which you might get dirty or sweaty.
- Keep earrings, bracelets, necklaces, rings, and other jewelry in an organized container to prevent them from getting lost, broken, eaten by a pet, or sucked up by the vacuum.

WHAT IS "GREEN" DRY CLEANING?

Over the past few years, there's been a boom in "natural," "green," and "organic" dry-cleaning businesses. While many of them operate in a more environmentally sensitive way than traditional establishments, there's no system of regulation or certification that guarantees they avoid toxic chemicals. If you're considering switching to a "greener" cleaner, ask the owners about the active ingredients they use to clean your clothes. The best methods are "wet cleaning," silicone-based cleaning, and carbon dioxide cleaning. If they still employ perc, don't waste your money by paying more for their services. Regardless of which dry-cleaning method you choose, it's in your best interest to employ it as infrequently as possible.

HOW TO MAKE FEWER TRIPS TO THE DRY CLEANER

- Wear an undershirt to keep sweat and odor from soiling your shirts and jackets.
- Get stains out as soon as they happen—don't wait until they're dried up and baked in.
- Hang clothes as soon as you take them off to prevent them from getting wrinkled, walked on, or soiled on the floor.
- Use a garment steamer to freshen clothes instead of cleaning them.
- Toss items in the dryer for 10 minutes with a damp washcloth to steam them.
- Use a lint brush to remove dust, dirt, or dander that may settle in over time.

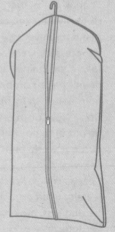

Dry Clean (Not) Only

The SHIFT: Some clothing labeled "dry-clean only" can actually be hand-washed in cold water and hung to dry without any damage being done to the garment. This includes sweaters (even cashmere), rayon, silk, and some wool.

Save $$: Up to $150 per year or more if you dry-clean the garment once a month.

Save the Planet: Perchloroethylene, or perc, the chemical used in most dry-cleaning operations, is listed by the U.S. Environmental Protection Agency as a hazardous substance to both human health and the environment.

Good for You: Long-term exposure to perc can cause liver and kidney damage. Perc is classified as a possible carcinogen.

Shift-it Tip: Professional cleaning is recommended for angora, fabrics with fancy stitching or embroidery, and structured or lined garments. After you pick up these items at the cleaners, remove the plastic covering protecting them and let them air out for five days or more before wearing them.

Make Over Your Clothes

The SHIFT: Repurpose or recycle old clothes instead of throwing them away.

Save $$: The savings are limitless if you're able to repurpose old items in a way that prevents you from ever having to buy new fashion—but will probably average about $100 per person per year.

Save the Planet: Save the resources used to make new items and keep your old threads out of the landfill.

Good for You: Redesign projects are a fun way to spend an indoor day with kids or friends.

Shift-it Tip: Use fashion magazines for inspiration.

Top Swap

The SHIFT: Instead of hitting the mall, throw a clothing swap party with friends.

Save $$: Up to $100 if everyone walks away with a new outfit.

Save the Planet: Conserve the resources and energy used to produce and transport new clothing.

Good for You: A swap is a great way to catch up with friends you haven't seen in forever.

Shift-it Tip: Anything left over can be donated to charity—and it seems only fair that the organizer gets the deduction! (A bonus: Many charities will pick up large donations.)

> **OVERDRESSED**
>
> Most people wear only about 40% of the clothes they own. Each year, Americans discard 690,000 tons of clothing, which breaks down to about 20 pounds per year for a household of four.

Just 'Cause

The SHIFT: Since most clothing is made overseas, look for clothes that are Fair Trade Certified or made by artisan-owned co-ops.

It's Worth It: Fair-Trade Certified clothing is more expensive than conventional clothing because it isn't made by grossly underpaid and overworked seamstresses. But because the quality is far better, your clothes will likely last longer, saving you from having to spend money on new items.

Save the Planet: Fair-Trade Certified clothing is more likely to be organic and less likely to involve the types of toxic chemicals and dyes associated with most garments made overseas.

Good for You: Feel good knowing that your money supported the health and well-being of people and their communities.

SWIFT SHIFT: RAG TRADE

If you thought barter went out with medieval times, you've never been to a cash-or-trade resale store. If you're jonesing for a "new" outfit but don't have any cash to spare, you can gather up some of your own castoffs and get ready to trade them for someone else's. That's exactly what our shifter Naomi did:

After a ruthless purging of the stuff in my closet, I had a few armfuls of pieces I knew I'd never wear again. So I headed to a local used-clothing store to sell my wares. A buyer inspected each garment I brought and selected the ones she knew she would be able to sell in her store. At first it irritated me that she passed on a few of my nicer items—I had some fab coats—but then I learned that they only buy clothes that are in season. So I'm going to store my cozier castoffs for a couple of months and make some more cash when the cooler weather comes.

She assigned each piece she was buying a retail price and offered me a percentage of the total retail sales my clothes would bring. I could take cash or, at a slightly higher rate of exchange, credit to shop the store's well-curated collection of seasonally appropriate merchandise. I would have probably given away the items to charity, so it was quite nice to get paid for them.

Naomi, Woodland Hills, CA
Married
Stay-at-Home Mother of Tydeman, 7; Jonesy, 5; and Poppy, 3

BEAUTY and PERSONAL CARE

Natural Beauty

The SHIFT: Buy organic cleansers, creams, and moisturizers that have been certified by the U.S. Department of Agriculture (USDA) instead of department-store brands with hard-to-pronounce cutting-edge chemicals.

Save $$: Up to $100 when you choose a 4-ounce organic product over a high-end label.

Save the Planet: USDA organic skin care products contain mostly plant-based ingredients that are grown according to organic standards. This means few (if any) chemicals associated with the product are harmful to the environment (although loopholes are always exploited).

Good for You: Skin care products that contain certified organic ingredients contain fewer synthetics that could harm you or your family's health.

Make Your Own

The SHIFT: Make beauty products at home from natural ingredients in your cupboards and refrigerator. After all, some people suggest that because you absorb whatever you put on your body, you shouldn't apply anything to your skin that you wouldn't eat.

Save $$: Up to $500 per year.

Save the Planet: Save the resources used to produce, transport, and package skin care products as well as the waste that is eventually generated when the empty plastic or glass containers are disposed of.

Good for You: Most conventional skin care products use chemicals that are potentially harmful to your health. By making your own concoctions from the ingredients you might put in a smoothie, you know you're doing your body good.

SWIFT SHIFT: WAKE UP TO NEW MAKEUP

Before I became a part of Shift Your Habit, I was a total beauty product junkie. I needed to figure out a way to save some money at the makeup counter, but I had no idea where to start. The beauty advice I received by being part of the Shift Your Habit project really opened my eyes to what I was actually putting on my face every day. It matters so much more than I had realized. With the new natural makeup, my skin just feels better. It's smoother and kissably soft. When I was using the old synthetic pore-clogging products, my skin felt irritated and dry. It certainly left me feeling less than my best.

Christin, Glendale, CA
Television Producer and Vintage Clothing Entrepreneur
Single, 28

Makeup Shakeup

The SHIFT: Instead of hauling around a makeup bag brimming with pencils and tubes, invest in some multiuse products. Why use a separate eye shadow, lip color, and blush when you can get all three in one skinny stick?

Save $$: Up to $100 per year compared with buying individual makeup products.

Save the Planet: Using half as many products means consuming half as much packaging. Many multiuse compacts are also refillable, which means even less waste.

BEAUTY PRODUCTS: WHAT TO PUT ON—AND WHAT SHOULD PUT YOU OFF

PUT ON

Plant-based ingredients
Instead of buying products with synthetic ingredients and potentially harmful chemicals, look for those with plant-based extracts and oils. Buy products from companies that have pledged to provide toxin-free products and that have signed the Compact for Safe Cosmetics. For the list of companies visit www.safecosmetics.org.

A short list of ingredients
Here's a case where "less is more." Look for products with the fewest number of ingredients. Avoid products containing phthalates, detergents, or antibacterial substances.

Minimal packaging
Look for health and beauty products with minimal packaging. Those that are made from recycled materials and that can be reused are best. If the packaging cannot be reused, try to buy containers that can be recycled. Where possible, opt for the largest container available. A single large bottle uses less energy and produces less waste than several smaller ones.

"Cruelty-free"
If you're concerned about animal testing, look for products certified by the Humane Cosmetics Standard (HCS)—identified by the "leaping bunny" symbol. HCS is the world's only international certification for personal care products that are not tested on animals.

"Ecocert"
This label, the USDA Organic seal, and the Organic Consumers Association (OCA) label indicate that your personal-care item contains organically produced ingredients.

PUT OFF

Antibacterial soaps
Use plain soap instead. It's equally effective at removing dirt and germs. Research suggests that triclosan, the active ingredient in

antibacterial soap, may not only lead to antibiotic resistance but might also in itself be harmful to human health.

Phthalates

This family of chemicals is used to bind fragrances in personal-care products. Phthalates are endocrine disrupters, which can cause premature birth, reproductive disorders, hormone imbalances, early-onset puberty, weight gain, and breast cancer. Avoid products containing the term *phthalate* or the acronyms DEP, DEHP, DBP, BBP, DIDP, DINP, or DNOP. Also avoid polyvinyl chloride (PVC) plastic, which contains high levels of phthalates.

Dyes and preservatives

Although they yield attractive colors and prolong your product's shelf life, they can be toxic to your body or cause allergic reactions.

Petroleum by-products

Moisturizers, hair products, foundations, lipsticks, and candles contain by-products of petroleum such as petrolatum, mineral oil, paraffin, and propylene glycol. Go for plant-based oils or beeswax instead.

Parabens

Like phthalates, these are a group of chemicals used widely in personal-care products as preservatives. Avoid products with ingredient lists that include any word containing *-paraben* (e.g., methylparaben, ethylparaben, propylparaben, or butylparaben).

LABELS TO QUESTION

If you see the term *biodegradable* or *natural* or *organic* or *botanical* on a beauty product label and it isn't accompanied by a certification seal, make sure you read the ingredients list before automatically assuming the product is healthy or eco-friendly. Such labeling on health and beauty products is not necessarily verified and implies no uniform standards.

DO YOUR RESEARCH

The Environmental Working Group has rated thousands of personal-care products for their safety. Check out its database at www.cosmeticsdatabase.com.

MAKE YOUR MAKEUP DO DOUBLE DUTY

Environmental issues aside, I hate having millions of beauty products hogging valuable real estate in my makeup bag. And if you think makeup containers are taking up too much space in your purse, you can imagine what they're doing to the landfill!

While any makeup junkie will tell you that women have been using lipstick as rouge for years, there are scores of cutting-edge products that have been developed with multiple uses in mind, so you can accomplish much more with much less (packaging and cash).

Just take a look at how easy it is to cut the number of products you use in half:

Replace eye shadow, lipstick, and cream blush with a three-in-one product in a neutral shade that suits your skin tone.

Turn in your moisturizer, foundation, and sunscreen for a tinted moisturizer with UV protection. Or trade your pressed powder and sunblock for mineral powder—which blocks solar rays naturally.

There's no need for separate blush and lipstick—just look for a lip and cheek stain and never worry about coordinating colors again!

And instead of investing in eye shadow, liner, and mascara, choose a stick that combines all three.

Nailing It

The SHIFT: Buy nail polish free of dibutyl phthalates and toluene instead of standard brand-name polish made with standard toxins.

Save $$: Up to $10 or more per year.

Save the Planet: Fewer toxic chemicals means reduced risk of damage to wildlife, fish, and ecosystems.

Good for You: Nail polishes are among the most dangerous cosmetics. Toluene is linked to cancer and both toluene and dibutyl phthalates are associated with developmental toxicity.

Smell Better

The SHIFT: Buy fragrance made from organic essential oils instead of name-brand perfume made from synthetic ingredients.

Save $$: Up to $30 or more per ounce.

Save the Planet: Essential oils made from organically grown herbs or flowers are free from the harmful chemicals used on conventionally raised flora, as well as from phthalates, which are associated with synthetic perfumes and fragrances.

Good for You: Certain phthalates are suspected carcinogens and can lead to hormonal and reproductive system disorders.

Kill the Dye

The SHIFT: Buy an at-home hair color kit instead of heading to the salon to get your hair dyed.

Save $$: Up to $1,500 per year.

Save the Planet: Save gas driving to the salon—assuming you buy your hair color kit when you're already at the drugstore.

Good for You: Most salons use chemically laden hair dyes that are potentially harmful to human health. One recent study reported that women who used permanent hair dye were twice as likely to contract bladder cancer as those who didn't color. When you do it yourself, you have the option of purchasing a hair color kit made with plant-based, nontoxic ingredients.

Bar None

The SHIFT: Buy a bar of soap instead of a plastic bottle of body wash.

Save $$: Up to $50 per year for a family of four.

Save the Planet: Reduce waste. Bars of soap are usually minimally packaged in recyclable paper or cardboard whereas body wash almost always comes in a plastic bottle.

RECIPES FOR GREAT SKIN

Your skin is your body's largest organ. And it happens to be very porous. This means that what goes on the outside of your skin is eventually absorbed into your body. Check out these recipes for gorgeous skin and huge savings—up to $350 per year compared with buying equivalent boutique-branded products containing natural or organic ingredients.

BODY SCRUB

Make this yummy, grainy body exfoliator in a cereal bowl. Pour about a cup of kosher salt into the bowl. Add just enough cold-pressed sweet almond oil to allow the salt to form moist clumps. It should stick together and be easy to pick up with your fingers. Add up to 20 drops of rosemary essential oil to scent the mix and invigorate the skin. (You can switch the rosemary essential oil for whatever you like best.) Store the scrub in a mason jar wide enough to fit your hand in, and massage over your whole body—not your face—in a warm shower.

Savings: Up to $160 per year compared with an organic exfoliant. Exchange salt rubs with a friend or partner and save an additional $90 compared with a salt scrub spa treatment.

FACIAL SCRUB

Grind 16 whole unbleached almonds and 4 tablespoons of oats in your blender, food processor, or coffee grinder. Don't blitz it for too long—you want bits big enough to slough off rough skin. Then mix the grit with 2 tablespoons of honey and about 4 teaspoons of yogurt or water—enough to create a loose paste—and gently pat into a clean face. Leave it on for ten minutes. Wet your hands to gently massage it into your skin. Splash your face with tepid water to remove. Use no more than twice per week and remember to follow it up with a moisturizer.

Savings: Up to $80 per year over a boutique-branded face scrub featuring almonds and oats.

LIP EXFOLIANT

A small glass jar—the size of an individual honey or jam pot at fancy hotels or restaurants—is the perfect container for this mixture. Mix 2 teaspoons of raw turbinado sugar—the brown kind—with 1 teaspoon of olive oil. The sugar is an excellent exfoliant, and the olive oil is moisturizing and full of antioxidants. Massage into your lips for thirty seconds using a light circular motion. This stuff is a great pick-me-up after a cold, when skin is dry and peeling. Don't forget to lick your lips afterward.

Savings: Up to $40 per year compared with a boutique-branded sugar-based lip exfoliant.

FACE MASK

Puree one avocado, 2 teaspoons of plain yogurt, and 2 teaspoons of honey in the blender, or mash in a bowl. Apply to just-washed skin. Avocado has healing qualities: It rejuvenates skin, soothes sunburn, and delivers a dose of antioxidants. Yogurt relieves sunburn and redness, and the lactic acid it contains helps hydrate and smooth. Honey soothes, heals, and nourishes, and some say it has antimicrobial, skin-clearing properties.

Savings: Up to $20 per year over a commercial organic facial mask.

FACIAL OIL

Combine 1 ounce jojoba oil with 1 ounce grapeseed oil. Add a vitamin E capsule and a few drops of lavender and neroli essential oils. Both grapeseed and jojoba oils are great for troubled skin types—neither will aggravate acne, but both are highly moisturizing. Apply after cleansing to moisturize skin.

Savings: Up to $50 per year compared with commercial blends made from essential oils.

If you have food allergies, please talk to your doctor before you try these recipes. Chances are, if it irritates the inside of your body, it will bother the outside as well.

Make Your Pouf Go Poof

The SHIFT: Use a washable washcloth or natural loofah instead of a plastic or nylon pouf.

Save $$: Up to $10 per year.

Save the Planet: Cut down on the plastic you use in your life, and reduce waste. Poufs aren't recyclable, so once they lose their luster they go straight to the landfill. Washcloths, on the other hand, are reusable for years and years.

SWIFT SHIFT: SPA AT HOME

As a single mom raising two teenage daughters in a small apartment, I don't have extra room in our budget for luxuries like beauty services, even though I'd love more than anything to give my girls the experience of being pampered at a day spa. So I was thrilled when Elizabeth offered us an opportunity to learn how to make our own spa treatments from ingredients that could easily be bought at the grocery store, saving us over $300 compared with getting individual facials at a day spa. It was not only fun but gave the girls and me a really nice opportunity to relax and learn together. I realize how important it is for my daughters to grow up using products that are as natural as possible, and preparing these recipes is a great way to teach them how to care for their skin. I think it's important for moms to know that you don't have to be rich to teach your daughters good skin care habits. Following a beauty routine doesn't just make you look better, it builds your self-esteem.

Nikki, San Fernando Valley, CA
Single, Mother of Casey, 16, and Cameron, 12

Razor's Edge

The SHIFT: Buy a rechargeable or plug-in electric razor instead of disposable razors or refillable blades replaced weekly.

Save $$: A total of about $80 per year—roughly the average cost of a decent electric razor.

Save the Planet: 1,000 gallons of water (no need to run the hot water when you have an electric razor); 150 pounds of carbon dioxide from water heating energy; and about 5 pounds of razors, packaging, and shaving cream container waste.

Good for You: Shaving with an electric razor tends to be much quicker than shaving with a disposable one.

Laser Sharp

The SHIFT: Invest in laser hair removal instead of waxing.

Save $$: Up to $2,500 over 10 years of hair removal treatment.

Save the Planet: The paraffin wax used for hair removal is derived from petroleum, which is a nonrenewable resource, while the electricity used during laser treatment is roughly equivalent to that of a standard lightbulb.

Good for You: Laser treatment can achieve permanent hair removal, whereas waxing must be done every five to six weeks.

Clean and Green

The SHIFT: Experiment with alternatives to traditional feminine hygiene products.

Save $$: A reusable latex or silicone menstrual cup, which costs $35 and lasts for five years or more, will save you up to $80 per year compared with disposable feminine hygiene products.

Save the Planet: Making this switch also keeps 300–350 fewer pads or tampons from being manufactured and entering wastewater treatment plants or landfills.

Good for You: There's no risk of toxic shock, or irritations from chemical bleaches or artificial fragrances.

Shift-it Tip: Other feminine hygiene product alternatives are non-applicator tampons and unbleached or organic cotton tampons—instead of the highly processed brand-name ones designed to look like little lipsticks.

HEALTH, BEAUTY, and FASHION: The Bottom Line

Make these shifts and save up to **$4,500** or more!

To share your experiences with low-impact fitness, vintage clothing, and homemade facials, check out **http://shiftyourhabit.com.**

MEET THE SHIFTERS:
Mary and Tom

Mary and Tom are retired—she from a career as a high school educator and coach and he from a career as a data specialist with a telephone company. They have been living green—without even knowing it!—for the last fifty years. They are an inspiration to me, and their lifestyle inspired many of the shifts in this book.

It's funny when Elizabeth refers to the way we live as "the gold standard," because we've been doing it this way ever since we can remember. Of course the environment is important to us, and of course we've always wanted to make every dollar we spend go as far as possible—but we really just want to live without waste.

In our home, for example, we try to limit our use of heating and cooling systems—so much so, that the gas company once thought we were stealing gas! They came and inspected all the lines, and suspected impropriety because of low usage. But all we were doing was being vigilant. It's really just about conserving, not living wastefully, and making the most of what we have. This philosophy of frugality and simplicity has allowed us to spend our money on things that we can really savor and enjoy, as opposed to writing a huge check to the utility company every month.

One of our greatest joys is traveling. We've been all over the world—to all seven continents. But when we travel, we aren't interested in touristy things. We really try to engage with and experience the local culture. We got remarried by a shaman in the Amazon and ate guinea pig in Thailand. In Wales, we had a typical dinner with a typical family in a typical home. In Sicily, we ate out in the farmland where our hosts grew their own vegetables. (We went to Antarctica, but we didn't get a dinner invitation from the penguins.)

Life is short—so it's important to have a spirit of adventure! It is never too late to keep challenging yourself with new experiences. I started doing New York's five-borough bike tour just six years ago. Mary enjoys exploring the open road in her Prius, and of course, we both love to travel. But you don't have to fly across an ocean or buy a hybrid to see the world in a new way. All you need is a pair of comfortable walking shoes. Take advantage of hikes and walks offered by national and municipal parks—many provide free guides. Just keeping our eyes—and hearts—open to the world around us is what keeps us feeling young.

Mary and Tom, Staten Island, NY
Retired Teacher and Communications Specialist

TRANSPORTATION and TRAVEL

I love traveling. And I've been lucky enough to do a fair amount of it, visiting big cities and tiny towns, majestic forests and fragile ecosystems. When I want to feel connected to the world and all the other people in it, I go on a trip. It may be a cliché, but by exploring the great unknown is how I've always found myself.

When finances are tight, the luxury of traveling is often the first to get cut from the budget. And nothing hinders travel plans like an increase in fuel costs.

In 2008, when gas soared over $4 per gallon for the first time ever, *staycation* became a buzzword—even though some wish it could be banned from the lexicon. A poll conducted in April of that year found that 40% of respondents were reconsidering their summer travel plans because of rising fuel prices. Some chose to drive shorter distances, others stayed away for fewer days, and some canceled trips entirely.

One of the things I love about the shifts in this book is that they put money back in your budget and give you the freedom to reallocate your finances in the way that's best for your family. So one idea might be to use some of the savings you'll realize by shifting your habits to reinstate the family vacation. This may mean camping in a national park instead of going to Europe or visiting an amusement park instead of driving cross-country. It doesn't need to be elaborate. It may just mean taking advantage of the art, culture, and entertainment that are available in your own backyard.

Or if you're fed up with having to pay a day's wage each time you stop at the fuel pump, you might consider investing in a car that gets more miles per gallon. Hybrids are surprisingly fun to drive. Their quiet hum is crazy! Even though I've been driving one for years, there are still moments when I have to ask myself if the engine is running.

Regardless of who you are or what you drive, this chapter contains dozens of easy shifts that leave a smaller footprint on the road and a smaller dent in your wallet—whether you're making your daily commute or making your way around the world.

VEHICLES

Gas Is Money

The SHIFT: Buy regular octane (low-grade) gasoline—unless your vehicle calls for premium fuel only.

Save $$: Up to $150 or more per year in gasoline expenses.

Save the Planet: For a standard engine, switching from premium fuel to regular unleaded gasoline results in more complete fuel combustion, which improves gas mileage and reduces smog-forming tailpipe emissions.

Think Small(er)

The SHIFT: Buy a fuel-efficient economy car instead of a standard sedan.

Save $$: Up to $7,000 or more on purchase price and up to $600 per year in gas costs.

Save the Planet: Economy cars may achieve up to 50% more miles per gallon than a standard sedan. This translates to an average of 150 gallons of gasoline saved per year, reducing greenhouse gas emissions by 3,000 pounds of carbon dioxide and less smog-forming exhaust out your tailpipe.

> **GAS GUZZLERS**
>
> According to the World Resources Institute, average gasoline consumption for motor vehicle transportation in the United States is 431 gallons per person per year, which is almost six times higher than per capita fuel consumption in Europe (73 gallons per person annually), and nearly thirty times higher than for developing countries (15 gallons per capita per year).

Good for You: Better gas mileage means fewer fill-ups—reducing the amount of time you're forced to breathe the fumes surrounding the pumps at the gas station.

Recharge Your Battery

The SHIFT: Buy a hybrid vehicle instead of an equivalent nonhybrid gasoline-powered vehicle.

Save $$: After the initial cost difference (which varies based on vehicle model and package but averages $6,000–$9,000 more for the hybrid), you'll save $600–$1,600 in gasoline costs per year.

Save the Planet: Saving 150–400 gallons of gasoline per year reduces your use of nonrenewable fossil fuels as well as your greenhouse gas emissions—a reduction of 3,000 to 8,000 pounds of carbon dioxide per year.

Good for You: Better gas mileage means fewer trips to the pump, which saves time. Federal tax credits may still be available for certain hybrid models.

Don't Diesel

The SHIFT: Buy a gasoline-fueled vehicle instead of an equivalent diesel-fueled vehicle.

Save $$: Up to $4,000 or more on initial vehicle price.

Save the Planet: Even though diesel cars get better gas mileage, diesel requires 25% more crude oil per gallon and produces 17% more emissions than unleaded gasoline. Also, diesel emissions are much dirtier than gasoline emissions, so they're greater contributors to unsightly smog, acid rain, and nitrification of water bodies. To date, all diesel engines are rated "inferior" by the American Council for an Energy-Efficient Economy.

Good for You: Because diesel uses more crude oil than gasoline and is more expensive to refine, it is prone to more extreme fluctuations in price. Further, not all gas stations offer diesel fuel, so filling up may be more of a chore. Diesel emissions are also known carcinogens, being found in some regions to account for 70% of the cancer risk from air pollution.

Veg Out

The SHIFT: If you already own a car with a diesel engine, opt for biodiesel fuel (either B20, which is 20% biodiesel and 80% petroleum diesel, or B100, which is 100% biodiesel) instead of standard diesel fuel (100% petroleum diesel).

Even $$: Depending on the price of oil, biodiesel can be a few cents cheaper or a few cents more expensive per gallon than standard diesel.

Save the Planet: Biodiesel is a renewable fuel made from vegetable oils instead of from nonrenewable crude oil. Biodiesel is associated with lower greenhouse gas emissions and less smog-producing pollution.

Good for You: Any diesel engine can run on biodiesel. No conversion kit is necessary, unless you're interested in making your own biodiesel from kitchen grease.

RULES of the ROAD

Not So Fast

The SHIFT: Don't speed. Driving over the speed limit can severely cramp your mpg.

Save $$: The difference between 60 mph and 80 mph is $900 in gas expenses per year (assuming 500 high-speed miles driven per month).

Save the Planet: 225 gallons of gasoline annually. On average, each 5 mph you drive above 60 mph lowers your gas mileage by about 2.5 mpg.

Good for You: In addition to the obvious reduced risk to your safety and driving record, sticking to the speed limit will also save you the time it would take for 15 additional fill-ups per year.

Choose Wisely

The SHIFT: If you have more than one vehicle—which is the case for most U.S. households—try to do the majority of your household driving in the vehicle that gets the better gas mileage.

Save $$: Shifting 5,000 miles of driving per year from your SUV to your economy car could save you more than $300 in fuel per year.

Save the Planet: Conserve up to 75 gallons of gasoline per year.

Plan Ahead

The SHIFT: Instead of hopping in the car each time you need to go to the bank, gym, grocery store, or school, try combining just three errand runs per week.

Save $$: An average of $220 per year on gasoline costs.

Save the Planet: Conserve 55 gallons of gas per year.

Good for You: Save on driving time—if it's city driving, you could save 50 hours per year or more.

Riding with the Wind

The SHIFT: Instead of cranking up the air conditioner on a warm day when you're driving at low speeds around town, roll down the windows and let the wind cool you.

Save $$: More than $160 per year on fuel costs, assuming about 25% of miles driven are at low speeds with the AC running.

Save the Planet: Conserve around 40 gallons of gas, as driving with air-conditioning can lower your fuel economy by as much as 4 mpg.

Good for You: Save the time it would take to pump an additional three tanks of gas per year.

Shift-it Tip: Because of the aerodynamic drag associated with having your windows open at high speeds, it's best to close the windows and turn on the AC if your speed exceeds about 45 mph.

Cruisin'

The SHIFT: Use cruise control when driving long distances on the open highway. Even if you think you drive with a steady foot, the smallest changes in pressure on the gas pedal can still eat up your gas dollars.

Save $$: Up to $70 on gas costs per year if you use cruise control for a quarter of the miles you drive per year on average.

Save the Planet: Cruise control can improve fuel economy by up to 14%, saving you about 17 gallons of gas per year if you use it for one-quarter of the miles you drive.

Good for You: When used safely, cruise control is also a great way to avoid speeding, which reduces your chance of being ambushed by the highway patrol and served a hefty moving-vehicle citation.

Shift-it Tip: Cruise control is not recommended for steep or windy roads, wet roads, or heavy traffic.

Idle Nonsense

The SHIFT: Limit the amount of time your car sits idle with the engine running.

Save $$: Up to $50 per year on gas costs by eliminating six minutes of idling time per day.

Save the Planet: Conserve more than 13 gallons of fuel per year—about an entire tank.

Good for You: Save the time it would take to fill up your gas tank once more this year. Also, if you're prone to using the drive-thru, it wouldn't hurt to stretch your legs and walk inside the coffee shop, pharmacy, or fast-food joint. You may even find that you're served in less time, which gets you back on the road sooner.

Don't Warm Up

The SHIFT: According to the experts, as long as your car was made after 1992 no warm-up is necessary. In fact, they say the best way to warm your engine is to drive it. And even in supercold weather, a 30-second warm-up should do the trick.

Save $$: Up to $45 worth of gas per year compared to warming up the car for an average of five minutes per day.

Save the Planet: Reduce gas consumption by about 11 gallons per year.

Good for You: Save the time you'd normally spend sitting in the car waiting for it to warm up—about 30 hours per year.

Lose the Weight

The SHIFT: Unload unnecessary cargo from your trunk. Driving around with tools, golf clubs, textbooks, or other heavy gear is a waste of gas and money.

Save $$: Nearly $25 per year for each 100 pounds of weight you re-move from your vehicle.

Save the Planet: Conserve up to 6 gallons of gas and 120 pounds of carbon dioxide. For every 100 extra pounds of cargo added to the vehicle, gas mileage drops about 1%.

Be Directed

The SHIFT: Instead of driving around needlessly when you're lost, consult a map or ask for directions.

Save $$: If you're prone to losing your bearings, you could save at least $20 per year at the pump by printing out directions be-fore leaving the house or asking for help as soon as you realize you're lost.

Save the Planet: Conserve 5 gallons of gas per year or more.

Good for You: Although we don't have an estimate of how much gasoline the typical driver consumes per year when lost, the guys on *Car Talk* once teased that "if every guy stopped and asked for directions when he got lost, the U.S. would never im-port another barrel of oil!"

MAINTENANCE

Fair Air

The SHIFT: Check and replace the air filter in your car regularly. Air filters keep impurities from damaging the inside of your engine and also help to maximize your fuel economy.

Save $$: Compared with driving around with a dirty filter, replacing it regularly could save you more than $240 per year at the pump.

Save the Planet: Improve gas mileage by up to 10%, reducing fuel consumption by 60 gallons or more per year.

Stay in Tune

The SHIFT: Get regular tune-ups. A car that's out of tune won't perform optimally, which means you'll get lower gas mileage than you'd see if your car was in tip-top shape.

Save $$: An in-tune car can save you $100 per year in fuel costs and thousands of dollars in repairs over time.

Save the Planet: Fixing a vehicle that's out of tune can improve fuel economy by 4%, or about 25 gallons of gasoline per year. Repairing a major problem—like an oxygen sensor in disrepair—can boost your mpg by 40%.

Good for You: Just like preventive health care, sticking to your scheduled oil changes and tune-ups can prevent your car from unexpected breakdown—and keep you from the unnecessary stress of having to rework both your schedule and your budget.

Under Pressure

The SHIFT: Check your tire pressure regularly and keep tires properly inflated.

Save $$: Nearly $80 annually on gas costs.

Save the Planet: Gas mileage can be improved by more than 3% just by keeping your tires inflated to the proper pressure, saving you almost 20 gallons of gas per year.

Shift-it Tip: Having underinflated tires reduces your gas mileage. But overinflating them does not give you even better gas mileage. It's best to stick to the manufacturer's recommendation for tire pressure.

Well-Oiled Machine

The SHIFT: Consult the experts—or your dusty owner's manual—about what type of motor oil you should be using in your vehicle. If you've been using the wrong grade of motor oil, switch to the recommended grade.

Save $$: Up to $50 per year.

Save the Planet: Up to 12 gallons of gas per year. Using the recommended grade of motor oil can increase gas mileage by 1% to 2%.

Good for You: Save the time it would take to fill up your tank once more per year.

Cap Happy

The SHIFT: Avoid driving around without a gas cap.

Save $$: Nearly $20 in gas costs per year.

Save the Planet: Missing gas caps cause gasoline to vaporize from the fuel tank, which results in harmful pollution and wasted gas.

COMMUTING

Go Public

The SHIFT: If possible, take public transportation.

Save $$: Up to $1,450 per year on gas expenses, plus an additional $2,250 in parking lot fees (assuming $9 per day—which is actually pretty cheap for most cities).

Save the Planet: Reduce gasoline consumption by 360 gallons per year and greenhouse gas emissions by more than 3.5 tons of carbon dioxide.

Good for You: Riding the bus or train to work can provide a good opportunity to do some pleasure reading, e-mail friends or colleagues, get caught up on the daily news, or cram for that meeting or presentation you put off until the last minute. If driving to work involves bumper-to-bumper traffic during rush hour, taking public transit can also cut significant time (and stress) out of your commute.

Work from Home

The SHIFT: If it makes sense given your job description and your company allows it, see if you can telecommute (work from home) twice a week or more.

Save $$: Up to $575 per year on fuel costs.

Save the Planet: Conserve 145 gallons of gas per year or more. That's ten fill-ups!

Good for You: Working from home cuts out your commuting time two days a week—which for the average worker would total 43 hours per year. And assuming you don't have to video-conference, telecommuting also allows you to skip the shower and work in your pj's if you so desire—saving an additional 100 hours per year.

Smart Wheels

Many people are intimidated by the idea of choosing a bicycle. Here's a guide to which two wheels are right for you.

Type	Best for . . .	Not so good for . . .	Cost
Road bike	Speeding along paved roads. Think Lance Armstrong.	Traveling with baggage or riding along uneven surfaces or dirt paths.	$700–$1,000
Mountain bike	Trudging along rugged or steep terrain at slower speeds.	Traveling long distances at a quick clip.	$200–$3,000
Hybrid	Riding paved streets or dirt bike paths. A commuter's bike.	Riding at high speeds or on extremely steep, rough terrain.	$300–$2,000
Cruiser	Leisurely rides on flat, even surfaces such as beach bike paths.	Traveling long distances, riding at high speeds or on steep or rough terrain.	$200–$700

SWIFT SHIFT: EVEN EASIER RIDER

My wife, Naomi, says that doing the right thing is contagious, and I guess my commitment to cycling proves her point. When we moved from London to California about eight years ago, one of the main criteria for determining which house to buy was that it be close enough to my workplace to allow me to bike to the office. This not only keeps me in shape for my bike races, it has allowed us to be a one-car family, and we're saving at least $450 per year in fuel costs alone.

Several of my colleagues have begun commuting by bicycle, and I'd like to say I'm partially responsible. (Seeing me arrive in one piece at the office each morning may have convinced them that they can, too.) These are people who had biked for pleasure before but who hadn't been sure they could manage the commute. Now they're total converts, recognizing that cycling is good for body and mind. A couple of them have mentioned that cycling has been like therapy—it has relieved stress and given them a chance to blow off some steam before walking through the door at home at the end of a long day.

For them, as for us, it's just icing on the cake that they're saving money. Elizabeth calculated that my co-workers and I are conserving a total of 500 gallons of gas per year—or about $2,000 worth! That's enough to add a pretty nice bike to our collection.

Rhys, Woodland Hills, CA
Senior Design Manager at a Mobile Communications Company
Married, Father of Tydeman, 7; Jonesy, 5; and Poppy, 3

Bike Right

The SHIFT: If you live within a few miles of your job, try biking to the office a few times per week.

Save $$: Up to $600 per year on fuel costs.

Save the Planet: Conserve 150 gallons of gasoline per year.

Good for You: Biking to and from work is a great way to get in shape and burn calories. It may also help you to decompress after a hard day at work.

Get Together

The SHIFT: Join a car pool or start a rideshare with two co-workers who live near you instead of each of you driving in alone.

Save $$: Up to $1,000 per year on gas.

Save the Planet: Together, you and your car-pool buddies will save 730 gallons of gas and more than 7 tons of carbon dioxide.

Good for You: Carpooling means you get to split the parking fees. If you normally pay $9 per day to park and you share the cost with two other people, you'll save an additional $1,500 per year!

Top Ten

The SHIFT: For some offices, it may be economical to have employees switch from working eight-hour shifts, five days a week to working ten hours, four days a week.

Save $$: Up to $300 per year on gas costs.

Save the Planet: Conserve nearly 75 gallons of gas annually. For an office of 25 employees, this translates to a savings of 1,800 gallons of gasoline and 36,000 pounds of carbon dioxide per year.

Good for You: Working a 4-10 workweek means you have a three-day weekend—every weekend!

PHONING IT IN

Today, roughly 45 million Americans choose to work from home or telecommute at least one day per week. This compares with just 11 million workers who reported telecommuting only ten years ago. If all Americans whose jobs allow them to work from home choose to telecommute just one day per week, collectively they could save nearly 850 million gallons of gasoline per year and reduce greenhouse gas emissions by more than 8 million tons. There also are electricity savings to be realized, as home office equipment uses less than half of the energy of commercial office equipment.

Staggering Genius

The SHIFT: If possible, stagger your work hours so that you commute during nonpeak times.

Save $$: Up to $250 per year on gas expenses.

Save the Planet: Driving at a constant speed instead of sitting in stop-and-go traffic can improve your gas mileage by 20% or more, saving approximately 65 gallons of gas per year.

TRAVEL

Travel Light

The SHIFT: Take an eco-tour instead of a standard or luxury tour.

Even $$: Prices may be comparable, but eco-tours are generally more affordable than luxury tours.

Save the Planet: Eco-tours are designed to minimize the environmental impact of tourism in terms of ecosystem disruption, waste production, and resource use. Focused on educating the traveler with respect to the natural environment and local culture, eco-tours intentionally support and provide financial benefits to local people and the local economy.

SWIFT SHIFT: BLENDING IN

When we go exploring internationally, we choose low-impact adventure travel tours in small groups, so we can get an authentic experience of the culture. Instead of staying in fancy hotels, we opt for home stays. Instead of white-tablecloth restaurants, we eat locally grown foods in the company of local people. You don't want to come out as the Ugly American. If you just want to eat hamburgers, stay home. We've heard that four-star hotels use twelve times as many resources as a single-star hotel. And obviously, they're thousands of dollars more expensive. By traveling the way we do, we're saving at least $4,000 per trip compared with taking a standard tour.

Mary and Tom, Staten Island, NY
Retired Teacher and Communications Specialist

No Excess Baggage

The SHIFT: Buy eco-friendly luggage (polyvinyl chloride [PVC]–free and made from water-resistant hemp, vegetable-tanned leather, canvas, organic cotton, or recycled materials) instead of luggage containing PVC plastic, waterproofing chemicals, virgin nylon or polyester, conventional leather, or nonorganic cotton.

Even $$: Prices may be comparable.

Save the Planet: Using more eco-preferable materials means luggage was made with less energy, fewer natural resources, and no toxic chemical inputs. Luggage made from recycled materials reduces the use of virgin materials as well as the generation of waste.

Good for You: Eliminating PVC, waterproofing chemicals, and other toxins means reduced risk of negative health effects for both the workers who made the luggage and the users.

Well Traveled

The SHIFT: Buy vintage or used luggage instead of new luggage.

Save $$: Up to $500 or more.

Save the Planet: Save the raw materials used to create a new product and prevent a used product from entering the waste stream.

Good for You: Luggage from decades past was often designed to be more durable than today's models. Much of it also features unique patterns, which can make identifying your suitcase at baggage claim a bit easier.

Carry On

The SHIFT: Pack a carry-on instead of checking your luggage.

Save $$: Given that most airlines are charging for checked luggage, you could save up to $30 per trip or more.

Save the Planet: Airlines charge for checked bags because additional fuel is used to transport additional weight. Packing lightly is an easy way to conserve fuel, which reduces greenhouse gas emissions.

Good for You: Traveling with just a carry-on saves you time checking in for your flight and picking up your bag at baggage claim, potentially giving you an extra hour on either side of your flight.

Free Refills

The SHIFT: Buy refillable travel-size toiletry bottles instead of disposable ones.

Save $$: Up to $40 per year. Travel sizes cost four times more per ounce than standard sizes.

Save the Planet: Reduce raw material production for packaging and reduce waste.

Good for You: Refillable bottles allow you greater flexibility in the types of personal care products you choose to travel with. The selection of travel-size products is limited to certain brands.

Door-to-Door Shuttle

The SHIFT: Take an airport shuttle service to and from the airport instead of driving yourself and using long-term parking.

Save $$: Up to $100 for a two-week trip.

Save the Planet: Sharing a shuttle with other passengers uses less fuel overall than if each of those passengers drove alone to the airport.

Good for You: The shuttle service will drop you off right at the terminal. You won't have to circle around the parking lot looking for a space or wait for the bus that picks you up from the lot and takes you to your airline.

Eco-Train

The SHIFT: Travel via Amtrak instead of by plane.

Save $$: Up to $50–$100 for regional trips.

Save the Planet: Amtrak runs an electric-diesel engine, which is 50% more fuel efficient than an airplane and produces fewer greenhouse gas emissions.

Good for You: Take in the landscape of the countryside, and enjoy more freedom to move about while you travel.

Good News

The SHIFT: Opt for a flight on a newer airline over a flight on an older, more established airline.

Save $$: Many newer airlines offer lower fares than the older ones.

Save the Planet: Newer airlines use newer aircraft, which are more fuel efficient and less polluting.

Good for You: Newer airlines often have features that improve passenger comfort and entertainment.

Lay-Under

The SHIFT: When possible, choose a nonstop flight instead of a flight with one or more layovers.

It's Worth It: Fares vary by airline, destination, flight time, time of year, and advanced booking. You may have a perception that nonstop flights are always more expensive, but this just isn't the case, especially if you plan ahead.

Save the Planet: Since a significant portion of the emissions associated with flying is discharged during take-off and landing, your carbon footprint will be lowest for flights with the fewest stops.

Good for You: Save the time and hassle associated with repeated boarding and deplaning.

Day Tripper

The SHIFT: Take a daytime flight instead of an evening one.

It's Worth It: Flight prices vary.

Save the Planet: Although there is no difference between day and evening flights in terms of carbon emissions, the warming effects of airplane contrails are twice as high at night because they continue to trap the earth's heat but do not reflect sunlight as they do during the day.

Good for You: Flying during the day may lead to a more restful night once you reach your destination, minimizing jet lag.

Greening Your Trip

Green vacations are much more affordable than you might think. And you don't have to book a special eco-tour to be green while traveling. Take a look at this comparison between a traditional and a green option for a ten-day family trip to Hawaii:

On the traditional trip, the family of four travels from Los Angeles to Honolulu to Kauai in a series of legs, for a fare of around $700 each. They stay at a high-end chain hotel in one room with two beds. They rent an SUV and eat all their meals at local restaurants or order room service.

On the green trip, the family flies nonstop from Los Angeles to Kauai, saving $160 per person. They rent a two-bedroom cottage with a full kitchen. They shop at the local market and cook most of their own meals. Since the property doesn't offer daily housekeeping unless the family requests it, the resort saves on water, electricity, and cleaning products and charges a much lower rate than the highrise hotel does. In fact, this green vacation costs half the price of the traditional one.

Here are travel savings, by the numbers.

	Regular Trip	Green Trip	Total Savings
Airfare	$670 per person	$510 per person	$640
Food	$140 per day for room service and dining out	$50 per day to cook in with local ingredients	$900
Hotel	$4,545 per 10-day stay	$2,045 per 10-day stay	$2,500
Rental car	$495 (SUV)	$300 (economy)	$195
Gas expenses	$180	$60	$120
Drinking water	$10 per day on bottled water	$0 for refillable bottles and tap water	$100
Activities	$1,500 for 90-minute helicopter tour, half-day backroads Jeep ride, sunset dinner cruise, scuba gear rental and lessons	$25 for self-guided hikes, sunset picnic on a hidden beach, body-surfing, boogie boarding, and snorkeling (using boards and snorkel gear provided free of charge at the rental cottage)	$1,475
Laundry	$180 for hotel laundry service	$0 for use of laundry facilities and detergents included with rental cottage	$180
TOTAL			$6,110

Be Near Now

The SHIFT: When booking your accommodations, try to stay within walking distance of the attractions you're planning to visit. Also make a habit of checking your accessibility to public transport.

It's Worth It: Although hotels downtown might be a bit more expensive, you can make up the extra expense by walking to attractions instead of having to rent a car or hail cabs.

Save the Planet: Conserve fuel and reduce pollution. For every gallon of gasoline consumed, about 20 pounds of carbon dioxide are emitted.

Good for You: Staying within walking distance of places of interest gives you the opportunity to stretch your legs and get some exercise. Skipping the rental car means you'll avoid the hassle of downtown traffic and the time and expense of finding parking.

Green Hotels

The SHIFT: If available, stay in a certified green hotel. Green hotels have made a commitment to actively reduce their impact on the environment.

Even $$: Prices can be comparable.

Save the Planet: Conserve water and energy, and reduce waste compared with a conventional hotel.

Good for You: Many green hotels use nontoxic cleaning products, offer soaps and shampoos without phthalates and parabens, and provide organic breakfast options.

STAYING GREEN ON-THE-GO

Whether you've chosen to stay in a green hotel or not, there are a number of ways you can still be green while living away from home:

Take short showers.

Turn the water off while brushing teeth and shaving.

Turn off lights and television when not in use.

Turn off the AC or heater when you leave your room or house.

Request that bedsheets not be changed during your stay.

Reuse your bath towel through multiple days by hanging it on the rack after use.

Leave any unused complimentary toiletries in the bathroom instead of loading them into your bag.

Home Away from Home

The SHIFT: If you want the comforts of home or have a large family or group you're trying to accommodate, consider renting a vacation home instead of staying in a hotel.

Save $$: Up to $3,500 on a three-bedroom house for two weeks compared with renting three separate hotel rooms.

Save the Planet: Staying in a vacation rental is just like living in your own house. Hotels, on the other hand, use excessive energy, water, and other resources to maintain daily housekeeping services, a 24-hour commercial kitchen, hallway lights, lobbies, etc.

Good for You: Most vacation homes come with fully equipped kitchens, laundry facilities, bedding, entertainment systems, etc. With the option to cook your own meals, you can significantly reduce your food expenses. And with in-unit laundry, you can justify bringing fewer clothes in a smaller suitcase. For family gatherings, vacation rentals provide both private sleeping quarters and common areas to spend time eating, relaxing, and hanging out together.

Shift-it Tip: Check out vacation rental opportunities around the world at www.vrbo.com.

Be Hostel

The SHIFT: Consider staying in a hostel instead of in a standard hotel.

Save $$: Up to $2,000 or more for a two-week trip compared with a hotel room.

Save the Planet: Hostels offer simpler accommodations than major hotels, using fewer resources to operate.

Good for You: Hostels are a great way to meet like-minded travelers. Many offer single rooms in addition to shared accommodations, so you have your choice if you want to have a bit more privacy.

Shift-it Tip: Check www.hostels.com for hostel accommodations in cities around the globe.

SWIFT SHIFT: HAPPY CAMPERS

When we travel domestically—which we did a lot when our kids were little—we camp in national and state parks instead of staying in hotels. On one five-week trip, we covered 8,000 miles in the United States—to Illinois, Kansas, the Dakotas, Wyoming, the Rockies, Texas; then back east through Tennessee and the Blue Ridge Mountains. We've calculated that traveling this way saves us up to $5,500 for a five-week trip and means we get to see natural wonders instead of touristy malls. And our kids, who are grown now with their own children, still talk about how much fun we had. Staying in hotels just doesn't create those types of lasting memories.

Mary and Tom, Staten Island, NY
Retired Teacher and Communications Specialist

Tent City

The SHIFT: Instead of choosing a vacation that involves staying in a hotel, consider pitching a tent in a state or national park.

Save $$: Up to $2,000 or more on accommodations for a two-week trip.

Save the Planet: Tent camping can be a great way to reduce the ecological footprint of your vacation and an excellent way to practice living with limited resources. Compared with a hotel, you'll save energy and water, and reduce waste.

Good for You: Experience nature. Get back in shape by going on a hike every day. Breathe fresh air. Stand in awe of huge canyons, waterfalls, lakes, mountains, wildlife, and meadows. Take fantastic pictures.

CAMPING TIPS

Stick to roads, paths, trails, and marked campsites.

Pack out your trash when you go on hikes.

Place campsite garbage in designated bins.

If your campsite has a bear box, USE IT!

Don't store any food or anything with a scent, or anything that looks like an ice chest, in your vehicle or tent. Bears and raccoons are smarter than they look.

Try to avoid using disposable products such as plastic utensils, Styrofoam, plastic bags, paper napkins, and paper towels.

Use biodegradable soaps and detergents.

Pour any soapy basin water in designated sinks, not into streams, rivers, or on plants.

Public Works

The SHIFT: If you're visiting a major city around the world, don't bother renting a car. Ride public transportation when it's available. Walk when it's feasible. And take a cab any other time.

Save $$: Up to $500 compared with renting a car. If you're traveling in Europe, your savings may more than double given the high price of petrol.

Save the Planet: Conserve the gasoline you would have otherwise consumed driving to your destinations (not to mention the gas you'll waste being lost).

Good for You: Public transit systems in most major cities are quite speedy and user friendly. As opposed to driving, taking the bus or subway keeps you from the frustration of trying to navigate the streets of an unfamiliar area—especially if in that area they drive on the wrong side of the road. It will also save you money on gas and parking fees.

Car Rental

The SHIFT: If you rent a car, look into renting a hybrid—or at least an economy car—instead of renting a full-size or midsize sedan.

Save $$: Up to $130 on gas for 3,000 miles of driving.

Save the Planet: Conserve 65 gallons of gas on your trip.

Good for You: Save the time it would take for an additional four fill-ups.

Memento

The SHIFT: Bring home locally produced, lightweight, sustainable, useful souvenirs that represent something unique about a region instead of cheap, useless, imported souvenirs—especially knickknacks.

It's Worth It: Prices vary, but anything useless is a clear waste of money.

Save the Planet: Useful souvenirs made from renewable resources (e.g., edible items, cotton or hemp clothing, artwork) cause little environmental damage and are less likely to end up being tossed during your next spring cleaning.

Good for You: You'll feel good knowing that buying locally produced items directly supports the people and economy of the place you visited.

BEFORE YOU LEAVE

Turn Off the Thermo—STAT!

The SHIFT: Make sure your heater or air-conditioner thermostat is switched to the off position before you leave on vacation.

Save $$: Up to $60 or more on energy bills compared with leaving the thermostat on for a month while you're gone.

Save the Planet: Conserve more than 550 kilowatt-hours of energy during the time you're away.

Cool Off

The SHIFT: It's useless to keep heating the tank of your water heater if there's no one in the house to use it. Most water heaters have a vacation setting for this reason.

Save $$: Up to $15 on energy costs for a one-month vacation away.

Save the Planet: 8 therms of natural gas or 150 kilowatt-hours of energy—keeping up to 100 pounds or more of carbon dioxide out of the atmosphere.

Unplugged

The SHIFT: Unplug anything in your home with a digital display, including clock radios, microwaves, DVD players, stereos, satellite receivers, etc.

Save $$: Up to $10 if you make this shift for a monthlong vacation.

Save the Planet: Conserve 100 kilowatt-hours of electricity—enough to run your television for 500 straight hours.

TRANSPORTATION and TRAVEL: The Bottom Line

Make these shifts and save up to **$8,500** or more!

For the greenest ways to get from here to there, and to share your journeys, visit **http://shiftyourhabit.com**.

MEET THE SHIFTERS:
Betsy and Daisy

Betsy, who teaches photography and runs her own jewelry company, is a single mom living with her four-year-old daughter, Daisy. They're in the process of renovating their house and they've chosen to live in a converted shed on the renovation site instead of moving to a temporary apartment or hotel. Living in close quarters with few luxuries—they don't even have a bathroom—not only has brought Betsy and Daisy closer but has also taught them that what really matters in life is not lots of fancy stuff but rather being together.

> *For the last eight months, my daughter, Daisy, and I have been renovating our house in the rural hills of Alta Dena, California. Our choice to remain on the property during construction has saved us both rent money and time traveling back and forth from one living space to the next. It's also enabled me to participate actively in the renovation process. Elizabeth estimates that we'll have saved over $11,000 by living on our own property instead of temporarily decamping somewhere else—not to mention the gas and electricity that would've been consumed had we chosen to maintain two places.*

I think the two of us living in the studio has been more difficult for other people to handle than it has been for us. (My ex-husband said he felt sorry for us!) But Daisy and I have loved it. It's true that living in a shed without a real kitchen—and with a college refrigerator—is not for the faint of heart. I sometimes go a week without washing my hair. I have to shop for food every day because we have no freezer. Living in the studio has made me very aware of efficiency, and I am much more discerning about every single item that passes through our front door, knowing that anything extraneous encroaches on our living space.

All this said, it's still really nice to live simply. I feel fortunate that I've been able to see how little I can really make do with. It's made me feel stronger. When you create a luxurious buffer, there's so much farther to fall. There's efficiency to living this way that's been really satisfying.

Part of our involvement with Shift Your Habit included planting an edible garden. I knew we'd probably get some tasty fruits and veggies out of it, but I had no idea how much quality time it would give me and Daisy. We now have another place to go together—which is especially nice when living in a tiny studio! The garden is a destination—we walk out there together and weed and pick and plant. It feels like a whole new room.

Planting an edible garden has proven to me that shifting habits improves more than just your household's bottom line—or your impact on the planet. It also enriches your life. Sometimes we forget—especially on the L.A. freeways!—that we are on this planet with other human beings, who, like us, have histories and fears and needs. We're really all in this together, and shifting our habits has taught us to stop and savor the rich and meaningful things and people in our lives.

Betsy, Alta Dena, CA
Artist, Jewelry Designer, Educator, Single, Mother of Daisy, 4

HOLIDAYS and CELEBRATIONS

It used to be that a great birthday party involved a homemade cake, some presents, and maybe a dip in some lucky kid's pool or a game of pin the tail on the donkey. These days the bar is set much higher.

Whereas just a generation ago, the idea of taking ten kids to the mall and letting them go crazy in the bulk candy store would've been considered over the top, now spending a few hundred dollars just to be relieved of planning, entertainment, and cleanup is considered a bargain.

Birthdays and other holiday celebrations are supposed to be designated as guilt-free quality time to spend with family and friends. But they can very easily run off the rails to become little more than an excuse to spend wild amounts of money, which results in crazy quantities of trash. When you think about getting ready for a holiday, your mind automatically starts making a shopping list, right? And chances are, most of the things you buy will end up in the Dumpster when the party's over.

You don't need a bunch of bells and whistles to have a great time—and your kids certainly don't, either. After all, a party is supposed to celebrate a person, not his or her stuff.

I didn't grow up with a lot of traditions, so holidays have gained meaning for me since I've become a mother. I love the idea of creating traditions for my son, Emmett, but I have to make a conscious effort not to focus them on things. I want Emmett's traditions to be built on shared experiences, not stuff. Like most of the shifts in this book, this has been easier—and more rewarding—than I had ever imagined.

Here are some simple choices that can help shift the focus away from frantic shopping and planning, and back to simply having fun together.

CELEBRATIONS

Get e-Vited

The SHIFT: Send electronic party invitations instead of mailing printed ones.

Save $$: Up to $20 per year on invitation and stamp costs.

Save the Planet: Saving paper conserves trees, energy, water, and waste.

Good for You: No need to spend the time shopping for the perfect invitation, writing out the details of the party, stuffing, sealing, and addressing envelopes or buying stamps. And online services keep track of the RSVPs for you.

Redecorate

The SHIFT: Buy high-quality reusable holiday and party decorations instead of disposable ones.

Save $$: Up to $100 per year.

Save the Planet: Most holiday decorations are made from paper or plastic that are neither recyclable nor biodegradable. Buying reusable decorations saves resources in the long run and reduces waste.

Good for You: No need to buy new decorations year after year.

Dispose of Disposable

The SHIFT: Use washable dishes, glasses, and silverware instead of disposable plastic plates, cups, and cutlery.

Save $$: Up to $25 per year.

Save the Planet: Using glass or ceramic dinnerware, which you likely already own, saves the resources used to manufacture the disposable varieties, as well as reduces plastic waste.

A Fine Vintage

The SHIFT: Instead of wrapping up a brand-new item, why not find a fashionable antique or used item of equally high quality?

Save $$: Up to $100 or more.

Save the Planet: Reusing things that other people have discarded keeps them out of the waste stream. It also saves resources on the manufacturing side, as fewer new products have to be made to keep up with demand.

Shift-it Tip: Do some investigation into the recipient's likes and dislikes and see if you can locate a hard-to-find toy, album, movie, TV show, piece of art, book, or other nostalgic item online.

Craft Services

The SHIFT: For any gift your child has to give, skip the expense of buying stuff and select a homemade craft that your child can help create.

Save $$: Up to $50 compared with a conventional gift.

Save the Planet: Conserve the resources used to manufacture a new product by choosing to make a craft out of nature-made or re-cycled items.

SWIFT SHIFT: SHIFT YOUR GIFT

Instead of exchanging holiday gifts, we donate to environmental organizations—but this mandate is not mandatory. My employees enjoy supporting the efforts of conservation groups. This also means that everyone's offices—and houses—will be just a little bit less cluttered with useless tchotchkes.

Brooke, New York City
Founder and Owner of a Creative Services Management Agency

UNSTUFFED

Instead of adding to the clutter that might soon become outdated and discarded, choose nonmaterial gifts for friends and family members. You'll save the energy and other resources that go into producing "things" and the waste associated with their eventual disposal. To boot, research shows that experiences can make people happier in the long run than material items. Here are a few ideas:

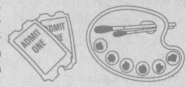

- Tickets to movies, theater, sporting events, amusement parks, TV show tapings, museums, concerts
- Gift certificates to restaurants, arcades, driving ranges, pottery studios, beauty salons, day spas, yoga studios
- Classes and lessons in art, cooking, language, fashion design, martial arts, music, sports, dance, horseback riding, surfing

Card Them

The SHIFT: Make your own card. Use your own words to tell your friend or loved one what he or she really means to you instead of letting a store-bought card say it all. You can make your own card with an online card creation program. If you have the time, you might break out the scrapbooking kit and make a card the old-fashioned way.

Save $$: Up to $50 if you typically buy 15 greeting cards per year.

Save the Planet: Conserve the resources (trees, energy, and water) used to make the card stock and envelope, and save transport energy, too.

Shift-it Tip: If you leave your card buying until the last minute, send an animated e-greeting online. You'll save the cost of the card and the stamp.

Rewrap

The SHIFT: Use wrapping paper made from recycled paper instead of high-end wrapping paper.

Save $$: Up to $5 per year.

Save the Planet: Gift wrap made from recycled paper not only saves trees, water, and energy but also keeps previously used paper out of the landfill. Also, most recycled wrapping paper is made with soy-based ink, which is nontoxic and rerecyclable.

Shift-it Tip: Enlist your kids to wrap gifts with you and get it done for free. Armed with brown paper bags, crayons, stickers, and scraps of leftover ribbon, kids can turn any package into a masterpiece, as well as make use of a lot of discarded materials.

THAT'S ENTERTAINMENT

Consider forgoing the clown, inflatable bounce house, pony, or fast-food-restaurant-hosted party in favor of a simple plan outdoors or at home. Check out the following high-impact party ideas with a low impact on the earth—and your budget:

- Borrow a projector from work or a friend, and screen a movie on your wall. Park the kids' toy cars in front of the screen for a drive-in.
- Throw a gardening party where kids can decorate a pot and plant a seedling.
- Host a mural-painting party.
- Open your own "beauty shop" and let the kids give each other makeovers (just hide the scissors).

BIRTHDAYS

Do Them a Favor

The SHIFT: Scrap the plastic-bag party favors filled with cheap plastic toys and candy in exchange for something kids make as a party activity.

Save $$: Up to $50 per year, depending on the number of party guests and contents of gift bags and prizes.

Save the Planet: The contents of party favors are usually made from plastic—which is a nonrenewable resource—and they're usually tossed within a week of being received.

Shift-it Tip: Here are some more waste-free favor options: books, iTunes gift certificates, seed packets, movie tickets, homemade baked goods or snacks.

Decorating Hero

The SHIFT: Skip the Mylar and latex balloons, foil banners and streamers, candy-filled piñatas, and other disposable flair.

Save $$: Up to $30 per year.

Save the Planet: Keep these nonrecyclable items out of the waste stream; they will sit forever in landfills or, worse, end up being mistaken for food by some unsuspecting bird, marine mammal, or other wildlife species.

Shift-it Tip: If decorations are necessary—that is, you're not having your party in a naturally festive setting like a park—choose ones that can be reused or recycled. Here are a few ideas:

- Cut letters for banners out of grocery bags and decorate with glitter, and then string celebratory messages over doorways.
- Color white flowers—carnations work well and are inexpensive—by placing them cut stem down in a glass of water spiked with natural food coloring.
- Project a cool image onto a blank wall with a slide projector.

- String fairy lights around windows year-round—don't just save their sparkle for Christmas.
- Buy some inexpensive paper lanterns and hang them from backyard branches.

END THE PAPER CHASE

So we managed to have a birthday party and use just one sheet of paper! I sent e-mail invitations to family and some friends and then printed off a single invitation that I posted at Cole's school. It felt so good not to buy paper invitations. It saved me at least $15 in card and stamp costs and probably an hour or more of stuffing and addressing envelopes. Plus, I saved all that paper!

Melissa, Huntsville, AL
Child Life Specialist
Married, Mother of Zoë, 12; Jackson, 5; and Cole, 4

Cake Walk

The SHIFT: Make your own birthday cake or cupcakes instead of buying either from a bakery.

Save $$: Up to $15 or much more.

Save the Planet: A cake baked in your kitchen involves less energy and fewer artificial ingredients than one made in a commercial kitchen. You'll also avoid having to recycle the large cardboard or plastic box used to transport the cake from the store to your house.

VALENTINE'S DAY

Feed Each Other

The SHIFT: Share a meal with your date on Valentine's Day.

Save $$: Up to $25.

Save the Planet: Either prevent food from being wasted, or avoid the burden of carting home an oversized foam to-go box that will inevitably be crammed into an undersized trash can.

Good for You: Room for dessert! And what's less romantic than the car stinking of garlic the next morning because you forgot to take in the leftovers?

In Bloom

The SHIFT: Buy organic roses instead of a nonorganic bouquet.

Save $$: If purchased online, organic roses may be up to $20 less per dozen than buying conventional ones from a florist.

> **BE MINE**
>
> Consumers spend an average of $100–$120 per year on Valentine's Day gifts and merchandise. Most people buy flowers, jewelry, greeting cards, or clothing.

Save the Planet: Since organic roses are grown without chemical pesticides, growers create an environment that attracts beneficial insects and promotes healthy plants. Farmworkers are not exposed to the harmful chemicals used on nonorganic flowers. You can feel good about supporting an organic greenhouse.

Good for You: Chemical residues stay out of your home as well as your nose—stopping to smell the roses shouldn't expose you to toxins.

Old Jewel

The SHIFT: Buy vintage jewelry or a custom piece made from pre-owned jewelry, instead of jewelry made from newly mined precious metals and gems.

It's Worth It: Prices vary.

Save the Planet: Buying or remaking used jewelry prevents the ecological damage caused by mining fine metals, diamonds, and other stones. Conventional mining uses huge amounts of water and energy, and results in cyanide-laced wastelands, contaminated drinking water, and decimated ecosystems. Vintage or remade jewelry does not support practices that exploit poor people around the world or funnel profits into organizations that fund violence.

EASTER

No More Plastic Baskets

The SHIFT: Buy well-made, Fair-Trade Certified Easter baskets instead of cheap plastic ones, and reuse them from year to year.

Save $$: Up to $10 per year.

Save the Planet: Save the resources used to make plastic baskets and the waste created when you throw them away.

Shift-it Tip: Weave your own baskets out of strips of paperboard (like cereal and cracker boxes) covered in fabric scraps or construction paper. Makes for a great craft during spring break.

Cut the Grass

The SHIFT: Use shredded paper as the "grass" for your Easter baskets instead of buying colored plastic grass. If you don't have a shredder, try using real grass or carrot tops.

Save $$: Up to $5 per year.

Save the Planet: In addition to being nonrecyclable, plastic Easter grass is unlikely to stay in the trash bin or at the landfill. If it blows away, it may be mistaken for food by a bird or marine creature and may seriously harm the animal. On the other hand, your shredded paper can easily be recycled after the holiday along with your other paper waste.

> ### EASTER MONEY
>
> Americans spend a total of over $14 billion per year on Easter, with the average household shelling out $135 for food, apparel, gifts, flowers, decorations, and candy. In all, nearly 80% of the population spends money on this holiday.

Rotten Eggs

The SHIFT: Avoid buying plastic eggs if possible. If you choose to buy them, make sure they're lead-free and that you store and reuse them from year to year.

Save $$: Up to $5 per year.

Save the Planet: Reduce the amount of plastic waste generated.

Good for You: Like other cheap plastic toys, plastic eggs have been found to contain lead. Lead is a known neurotoxin that can impair brain development and the nervous systems of children.

HALLOWEEN

Ghosts of Halloweens Past

The SHIFT: Buy or rent costumes from a vintage shop or thrift store instead of springing for a new Halloween costume—especially a plastic one.

Save $$: Up to $25 per year.

Save the Planet: Conserve the resources, energy, water, and chemicals that would have been used to make and transport a new costume.

Shift-it Tip: You don't have to spend any money at all to outfit the family for Halloween each year. Offer to host a family or neighborhood costume swap: Arrange all the hand-me-downs as though they were in a store, and let the kids go "shopping." You can also throw a party and require guests to make their costumes from stuff they were planning to throw away. Offer a prize for the most creative costume.

> ### TRICKS AND TREATS
>
> Halloween is the second-biggest consumer event in America, after Christmas. Nearly two-thirds of Americans celebrate Halloween each year.

SWIFT SHIFT: COSTUME CHANGE

On Halloween, despite my husband's protests, we celebrate by dressing up the boys. I try not to buy costumes. Instead, I make them myself or use this great trick: I buy character pajamas for my smaller son, which make an ideal (and reusable) costume. He doesn't know the difference, and we don't throw his outfit out when the night is over.

Melanie, Los Angeles, CA
Middle School Teacher
Married, Mother of Miles, 10, and David, 5

Bag It

The SHIFT: Give your kids a reusable canvas bag instead of buying them a new plastic pumpkin pail every Halloween.

Save $$: Up to $10 per year.

Save the Planet: Plastic pumpkin pails are made from petroleum, a nonrenewable resource. When thrown away after they've outlived their usefulness, they live on in the landfill for thousands of years.

Shift-it Tip: For the same price as a plastic pumpkin—around $3— you can purchase a blank canvas bag for your child to personalize. Just fashion a cut potato into a stamp shaped like a pumpkin and give your child a saucer full of orange fabric paint.

THANKSGIVING

Pass Up the Plastic

The SHIFT: Use natural decorations like dried corn, gourds, pumpkins, and maple leaves instead of disposable plastic decorations.

Save $$: Up to $20 per year.

Save the Planet: Natural decorations are renewable resources whereas most manufactured decorations are made from plastic—which is produced from petroleum. Disposable decorations inevitably end up as garbage after the season has ended.

Good for You: Natural decorations can create a much less commercial-looking atmosphere. If they're fresh and edible gourds or pumpkins, they can be cooked and eaten after the holiday.

Turkey Winner

The SHIFT: Unless you're serving an army, or are planning to repurpose the leftovers, buy a small turkey (10 pounds) instead of an XXL turkey (20 pounds).

Save $$: Up to $10 per year.

Save the Planet: Raising smaller turkeys consumes fewer resources in terms of food, land, and water, and it produces less waste and requires less energy for transport.

Good for You: Smaller turkeys cook faster than large ones. You'll save an average of about ten minutes of oven time per pound. They also take up less space in the fridge and result in less carcass waste you have to throw away.

CHRISTMAS

Green Tree

The SHIFT: Buy an organic live (or living) Christmas tree, instead of an artificial tree.

Save $$: Up to $100 over the average 6-year lifetime of an artificial tree.

Save the Planet: Live (or living) trees are renewable resources, requiring only soil, sun, nutrients, and water to grow. Artificial trees are typically made in China from polyvinyl chloride (PVC) plastic, which is produced from petroleum and associated with toxic pollution from production to disposal. Live trees don't require space for storage and can easily be composted after the new year.

Good for You: PVC plastic is linked to cancer-causing dioxin, and the average plastic tree contains nearly 70 grams of lead.

HOLIDAY CASH, HOLIDAY TRASH

Yuletide revelers spend about $830 per year on holiday shopping, and 40% of these consumers begin their buying spree before Halloween. Gift giving makes up the largest portion of the holiday budget, with the average consumer spending $625 on gifts for family, friends, and co-workers. It's estimated that an extra one million tons of waste is generated every week between Thanksgiving and New Year's Day.

Light Bright

The SHIFT: Buy light-emitting diode, or LED, miniature holiday lights
instead of the incandescent variety.

Save $$: After the initial price difference (LED lights cost about $5 to
$10 more per 100-light string), save $3.50 per holiday season
on energy costs and $50 on replacement light strands over
their 20-year lifetime.

Save the Planet: LED lights use about 10% of the energy consumed
by incandescent lights. LED lights are made to last for up to
100,000 hours—nearly 50 times longer than incandescent
lights.

SWIFT SHIFT: EVER GREEN

*Ever since Daisy was born, we've made an effort to plant
our Christmas tree after the season is over instead of throw-
ing it away. We've had all different kinds of trees in our
different backyards, but what's remained consistent is that
Daisy believes that a tree is a living thing—something that
needs to be nurtured, not trashed. I can see these beliefs
spilling over to the way she treats our edible garden—she
always wants to check on and encourage the plants, almost
as though they were her pets. I'm really proud that Daisy
shows so much respect to the natural world around her.*

Betsy, Alta Dena, CA
Artist, Jewelry Designer, Educator
Single, Mother of Daisy, 4

NEW YEAR'S EVE

Fun for Rent

The SHIFT: Rent glass champagne flutes instead of buying plastic champagne flutes.

Even $$: Prices can be comparable.

Save the Planet: If you don't have your own stash of champagne flutes, renting champagne glasses from a local party supply rental company is the ultimate way to help the planet. You reduce the amount of resources needed to make new flutes (either glass or plastic) and avoid having to toss a full trash bin worth of plastic flutes.

Good for You: There's nothing like the tone of a toast with glass champagne flutes—they sure beat the flat click of plastic. And they're way less tacky.

CELEBRATIONS and HOLIDAYS: The Bottom Line

Make these shifts and save up to **$700** or more!

To celebrate all your green parties by sharing with other shifters, and for more party guides, visit **http://shiftyourhabit.com.**

AFTERWORD

I hope you'll think of this book as your toolkit for success. Whatever you do, don't leave it on your bookshelf. Toss it on your kitchen counter, keep it on top of your desk, stuff it into your gym bag or purse—take it wherever you'll use it. Make it a guide to simplify all the choices you make in your daily life. When you do, you'll see that small shifts really do add up to big change.

When you think of your life as a series of small, conscious decisions that you control, you begin to feel hopeful instead of hopeless. Suddenly, it's clear that the only way to accomplish big things is to commit to taking small steps. And when you look around and see that so many others have decided to do the same, you'll find that it's exhilarating to get in on the beginnings of something major. You'll be at the heart of a growing community striving to change the world. You'll realize that your actions really do matter.

While there are hundreds of shifts in this book, I realize we've barely scratched the surface when it comes to thinking about smarter ways to live. The Shift Your Habit philosophy, with its timeless emphasis on efficiency, applies to every aspect of your life. Once you internalize this point of view—that you truly can have everything that matters while giving up very little—you'll be coming up with shifts of your own.

The success of this movement depends on you and your willingness to participate in a global game of eco-telephone. I am counting on everyone who reads this book to make a shift and pass it on. Encourage your kids, your parents, your students, your teachers, the members of your mom's group—and your book club—to do the same. Share your successes—and your botched efforts. Use these ideas as an opportunity to connect with people in your community. Work together to take your shifts to the next level.

Now that you know that living green doesn't mean spending green, you don't have to feel self-conscious about spreading the word. Maybe your neighbors are wondering why your garden suddenly looks so lush, why you're biking to work, why you're sweeping—instead of hosing down—your driveway. Tell them! By sharing ways to turn less into more, you can make a real difference for yourself, your family, and your world. Everywhere you look, you'll see proof that, contrary to the popular maxim, people *can* change.

Shifts happen.

Share yours with us at http://shiftyourhabit.com.

ACKNOWLEDGMENTS

Shift Your Habit would not have been possible without the wonderful families that started this movement with me. I am eternally grateful for your time, trust, and stories, and I am so happy to have so many new friends. Many thanks to GE, PUR, Fleurville, and Shaklee for their support in getting the families started with their shifts. You added huge value to their experience. Thank you to my wonderful experts for their time and information: Christy Coleman, eco-makeup artist and green beauty expert; Jeanne Kelley, author of *Blue Eggs and Yellow Tomatoes* (my favorite cookbook; see www.jeanne kelleykitchen.com/Site/Home.html); Catherine McCord for her unbelievable homemade baby food recipes, she's a genius and a beauty (http://weelicious.com/); Gina Monaci of Smartscape edible gardens for planting and teaching us so much; Joanne Moore, the incredible chef of Axe restaurant; Christopher Kosloski, my genius travel expert, who always looks at all sides of travel for the best solution; and Bud Fallon for his workout tips galore. To my team, for which a thank-you cannot express how much you mean to me and how much I value and appreciate the hard work and effort that went into this book: Adee Pelleg, Ingrid Franz Moriarty, and Monica Rivera. And for their support and guidance: Matti Leshem, Cameron Diaz, Aaron Kanter, Tommy McGloin, Alex Drosin, Richard Pine, Mary Choteborsky, Philip Patrick, Eric Hirshberg, Chad Saul, Jon Ritt, the Deutsch design team, Mary Ann Marino, Christy Beck, Elaine Ornelas, Joe Blake, Shannon Garbiero, Linda Meltzer, Jennifer Sbranti, Jesse Lutz, and Josh Baran (Soda Stream!). My love and shifts to you all.

INDEX OF TIPS

About the Authors

Elizabeth Rogers is a bestselling author, environmental consultant, and entrepreneur who is committed to helping people make an impact on their world. In 2007 she coauthored *The Green Book: The Everyday Guide to Saving the Planet One Simple Step at a Time.* A *New York Times* bestseller, *The Green Book* has been translated into ten languages. Every day she tries to shift a habit to support the global green effort. To learn more about her daily shifts, log on to **http://shiftyourhabit.com**.

Colleen Howell, Ph.D., serves as the primary researcher and content manager for Shift Your Habit. She is an environmental science writer, eco-solution designer, and sustainability consultant.